RAF Hunters in Germany

Front Line Defenders in the Cold War

Günther Kipp & Roger Lindsay

Printed in the United Kingdom. A catalogue record of this book is available from the British Library.

ISBN 0-9544069-0-7

The Authors welcome additional information relevant to this book and may be contacted in writing at the following addresses:
Günther Kipp, Im Obstgarten 18a, D27798 Hude, Germany.
Roger Lindsay, 7 North Meadow, Hutton Rudby, North Yorkshire, TS15 0LD, England

Photographs on preceding pages
Cover 122 Wing Leader, Wg Cdr C.S. 'Hammer' West flew his personal Hunter F.4 XE665 in 1955/56, and decorated it with the markings of the four component Hunter squadrons at Jever which comprised the Wing Nos.4, 93, 98, and 118, which can be seen in miniature beneath the cockpit, together with his Wing Commander's rank pennant.(Brian Sharman)

Inside Front Cover
Three generations of 4 Sqn Hunters in Germany: (Top) F.4 WV275 'D' being flown by the C.O. Sqn Ldr Ray Chapman, whose 'personal' aircraft 'Alpha' happened to be unserviceable when the picture was taken. (Centre) F.6s began to replace the F.4s from February 1957 and in this Jever flight line picture taken the following year the much reduced size of the squadron markings is evident. XE548 'H' incorporates Mod.228 - the extension of the outer wing leading edge - while XG298 'X' has yet to be so modified, and neither carries under wing drop tanks although fitted with the pylons to accept them. (the late Dick Millward) (Bottom) Hunter FR.10 XE585 at Gütersloh in February 1969 with its full complement of 230 gal.(inner) and 100 gal.(outer) drop tanks. The colourful squadron markings have now been restored to the fuselage as well as the nose, which carries the name of the C.O. Sqn Ldr A.J.Hopkins, together with his rank pennant beneath the cockpit. (E.Westersotebier)

This Page
XE665, the same aircraft as illustrated on the cover, but now seen soon after its transfer on 17 April 1956 to 118 Sqn, coded 'A' and assigned to the C.O. Although actually being flown on this occasion by Flt Lt Ken Goodwin (MOD)

CONTENTS

Introduction

In the spring of 1955 a new shape started appearing in the skies above the North German Plain. Although the sight of swept wings - in the shape of RAF Sabre 4s - was not an unfamiliar one, the graceful lines of the Hawker Hunter with its skilful blending of fuselage, air intakes and wings and the unique shape of its fin were something quite different. It seemed to look more like an exercise in airborne aesthetics rather than a combat aircraft with the lethal power of 4 Aden guns, which is how it would probably have appeared to the crew of a Soviet TU-16, an encounter which was fortunately destined never to occur.

It took little more than a year to re-equip 13 squadrons with Hunter 4s, grouped in 4 Wings and based at the RAF stations at Jever and Oldenburg on the North German Plain as well as at Brüggen and Geilenkirchen in the Rhineland close to the Dutch border. Ten of the squadrons had previously flown Sabre 4s whereas three had been equipped with Venom FB.1s. This was no mean achievement, even when measured by the standards of the fifties, and put into perspective it meant that when the re-equipment programme was completed by the middle of 1956 there were as many Hunter squadrons based with the 2TAF in Germany as there were with Fighter Command in the UK.

We consider that this is sufficient reason to produce another publication on a subject which, although previously covered, has been inadequately dealt with as far as the operations of Hunters in Germany are concerned, leaving many unanswered questions and consequently lacking the detail which it deserves. This publication aims to remedy the situation by looking briefly at the position of the Royal Air Force in Germany from immediately after the war to the end of the Hunter fighter era in 1971, explaining the reasons behind the fluctuations in strength in terms of numbers of squadrons deployed during that time and obviously concentrating on the Hunter as the last example of a dying breed - the day fighter and to a lesser extent, its reconnaissance version, while not neglecting the trainer versions, which soldiered on until the mid -1980s. The composition of the fighter wings which controlled the squadrons, their activities, plus supporting facilities such as GCI radar stations and firing ranges are all explained. Photographic coverage is extensive, and the great majority of images are published for the first time, and support the detailed information on unit markings.

The development of the Hunter and details of its technical specification have been exhaustively dealt with in previous publications, and these aspects are therefore only touched on in this publication so long as that contributes to a better understanding of the subject.

Acknowledgements

With the heyday of the operational career of the Hunter fighter peaking over forty years ago, it is obvious that the amount of literature devoted to it is immense, and therefore authors who tackle the subject so many years "after the event" are bound to benefit from previous publications, and we would like to express our special thanks to the following writers: Anthony J.'Bugs' Bendell, Roy Braybrook, C.G. Jefford, Francis K. Mason, Hans Onderwater, W. J.(Bill) Taylor and Nigel J.R. Walpole.

The help of those pilots who served on the Hunter squadrons (or controlling wings or flying support units) in Germany has been vital in the compilation of this book, be it in the form of general information, their own experiences with the aircraft, or the provision of photographs, and has immensely contributed to its authenticity. In this context we are particularly indebted to Dick Barraclough, B. B. Batt, Charles Boyack, Robin A. Brown, Gordon B. Browne, Alan Chapman, the late Ray Chapman, Alan C. East, Ken J. Goodwin, Mike Hall, Danny Lavender, Ron Ledwidge, Mike McEvoy, E.L.'Peter' McMillan, the late Dick Millward, Paddy Minnis, Derek Morter, Ralph Owen, David L.Parsons, Alan R.Pollock, Peter Raeburn, Mick Ryan, Peter Sawyer, Brian B.Sharman, J.Brian Thornton, W.(Bill) R.Toosz-Hobson, Nigel J.R. Walpole, and Chris Wilmot, as well as to The Hunter Operational Register (THOR)… and we hasten to add that no disrespect is intended by using their Christian names rather than their service rank, while recognising that most were very young, comparatively junior pilots during the Hunter era, although some subsequently attained senior rank.

Similarly we wish to acknowledge the generous assistance given by our fellow researchers and Hunter enthusiasts, most of whom have been close friends for many years, including: Bruno Albers, Gerd Behrendt, Jurgen Breuer, Tony Buttler, Peter Caygill, Geoff Cruikshank, Michael Drechsler, Paul Fehlauer, Norbert Giese, Peter Green, Günther Hindersmann, Joe Hooker, Klaus Kropf, Walter Lewecke, Heribert Mennen, Wolfgang Mennen, Wilfried Moll, Tom Morton, Charly Pfeiffer, Robbie Robinson, Axel Saal, Dieter Schmidt, Phil Spencer, Ray Sturtivant, Andy Thomas, Dick Ward, Erich Westersötebier, Heiko Weichardt, Wilfried Zetsche, and Wilfried Zucht.

Almost 50 years ago, when most of what is described took place, photography, especially of military aircraft, was a rather rare pursuit and, when "conducted" from over the fence outside RAF airfields, was not always regarded as an innocent activity, and was frequently viewed by the police with some concern; also the rather basic equipment of those days sometimes made it difficult to take good quality photographs. With this in mind, our thanks go to those who persevered, inside and outside the fence and made it possible that those activities of half a century ago can not only be described but also documented here in visual form. The source of those photographs has been acknowledged in the captions to each picture, however sometimes their origins, for various reasons, are obscure and this may have led to incorrect credits; *If we have inadvertently omitted any contributor we hope they will accept our profuse apologies!*

Günther Kipp and Roger Lindsay
May 2003

Dedicated to the air and ground crews who lost their lives in the course of RAF Hunter operations in Germany.

Hunter FR.10 XE556 'W' of 2 sqn after take-off from RAF Gütersloh in May 1969. (Günther Kipp)

The Royal Air Force in Germany from 1945 - 1971

As could be expected, the end of the Second World War did not result in an immediate reduction in the size of the Second Tactical Air Force. When being renamed British Air Forces of Occupation (BAFO) in July 1945 it comprised 4 Groups, 20 Wings and 68 Squadrons which were based on some 20 airfields in Germany and The Netherlands.

Due to changing peacetime requirements and also the state of Britain's weakened economy, the pace of disbandments of units accelerated so that by the end of 1947 BAFO had just 10 squadrons at its disposal, which were based at Wunstorf near Hannover (1 squadron of reconnaissance Spitfires and 2 squadrons of Tempest Vs), Gütersloh (3 squadrons of Tempest IIs) and Wahn near Cologne (4 squadrons of Mosquitos). It is worth noting that at that time there were no night fighters based in Germany, a situation which was only remedied with the arrival of 4 squadrons of Meteor NF.11s in 1952.

When in June 1948 the Soviet authorities closed all surface links to Berlin, situated in the middle of the Soviet Zone of Occupation, aircraft of the RAF and the USAF supplied the city with essentials until May 1949, when the blockade was lifted.

The blockade of Berlin and the outbreak of the Korean war in June 1950 obviously fundamentally changed the assessment of the Soviet threat and an expansion programme for BAFO was the consequence.

This expansion programme went on right across NATO. For the RAF in Germany it meant first and foremost the reactivation of ex-Luftwaffe airfields at Bückeburg, Celle, Fassberg, Ahlhorn, Oldenburg and Jever and the construction of new airfields - the so called "Clutch" airfields - at Wildenrath, Geilenkirchen, Brüggen and Laarbruch, which opened between 1952 and 1954.

In terms of aircraft, Vampire day-fighters arrived first and were based at

Business end of a Brüggen-based Hunter 4 wearing the famous 'Sharksteeth' markings of 112 Sqn. Brand new in the spring of 1956 this aircraft has yet to acquire its individual aircraft code letter on the nose wheel door. (Robin Brown)

Celle, Fassberg, Wunstorf, Gütersloh, Ahlhorn, Oldenburg, Jever, Wahn, Brüggen, and Wildenrath, followed by Meteor NF.11 night fighters at Ahlhorn and Wahn. Venoms replaced Vampires at Celle, Fassberg and Wunstorf and Geilenkirchen started with Sabre 4s. Reconnaissance Meteors went to Bückeburg and Gütersloh.

While this was all going on, BAFO, no longer an air force of occupation, changed its name to Second Tactical Air Force in September 1951.

As the USAF had found out in Korea, their F-86s were - in the hands of experienced pilots - more than a match for the Soviet Mig-15s. The same, though, could definitely not be claimed for RAF Vampires and Meteors. This fact and the assumption that some 500 Migs were based just across the border in East Germany led to the decision to buy more than 400 Canadair Sabres as a stop-gap before the Hawker Hunter became available. Sabres started replacing Vampires from March 1953 and eventually equipped 10 squadrons on 4 airfields as well as - temporarily - an OCU at Wildenrath.

The unfolding of the re-equipment programme continued with the deployment of 4 squadrons of Canberra B.2s at Gütersloh, only some 70 miles from the border with the GDR, and under the operational control of Bomber Command, as there were insufficient airfields available in the UK at that time to accommodate all the Canberras coming off the production lines. 4 squadrons of reconnaissance Canberras followed at Laarbruch and Wahn and were later reduced to 3. Hunter 4s started re-eqipping first Venom and subsequently Sabre squadrons in April 1955 and by the middle of 1956 there were 13 squadrons based at Jever, Oldenburg, Brüggen and Geilenkirchen. Also in 1956, two squadrons of Swift FR.5s had replaced Meteor FR.9s and PR.10s, the Canberra

wing at Gütersloh had been disbanded and the deployment.Thent to Germany of strike Canberras had begun.

With 36 squadrons deployed, 1956 proved to be the post war climax for the RAF in Germany, but this state and high morale among servicemen and women was not going to last for long!

By 1957 defence planners had obviously come to the conclusion that as it was impossible to guarantee 100% defence against incoming nuclear bombers and ballistic missiles it did not make any sense to maintain an unnecessarily large fighter element. Nuclear deterrence was therefore to guarantee national security and the deterrent forces were to be defended by a relatively small number of fighter units. This led to the infamous Duncan Sandys White Paper on Defence and resulted in a watershed for the RAF as a whole with 2TAF in Germany being no exception.

The result was dramatic: 9 Hunter and 6 Venom squadrons were disbanded in 1957 and the airfields at Bückeburg, Celle, Oldenburg, Wahn, Wunstorf and Ahlhorn handed back to the Luftwaffe in 1957 and 1958. One Hunter 6 squadron was reformed by the middle of 1958 thereby bringing the Hunter force to 5, based at Jever and Gütersloh. In 1959 the command was renamed RAF Germany and by 1961 when Jever was also handed over to the Luftwaffe, squadron strength had fallen to just 12 and this was to be the figure maintained over the coming decades.

The re-equipment programme of the 1957 White Paper was translated into the arrival of Javelins to replace the obsolete Meteor NF.11s. Also it brought the end of a dying breed: the day fighter. 4 Hunter 6 squadrons were disbanded by the end of 1960 while the last one soldiered on for another two years. Of course this was not the end of the Hunter. The Swift FR.5s had been replaced by Hunter FR.10s in 1960/61 and these were going to stay right through the sixties.

To complete the picture to the early seventies, one arrival deserves a special mention: the long overdue introduction of the supersonic Lightning. Two squadrons of F.2s replaced the Javelins from 1965 and were based at Gütersloh and Geilenkirchen. From 1968 they were modified to F.2a standard and operating from the same base - as Geilenkirchen had closed down - at Gütersloh. After a long and very useful life in Germany, the Canberras gave way to four squadrons of Phantoms in 1970, one of which was earmarked for the reconnaissance role, and two of Buccaneers in 1971. This brief history will not be complete without mentioning the unique Harrier, which started its long and still ongoing service career in 1970.Three squadrons were eventually based at Wildenrath. The Harrier seems set to become the combat-type with the longest service history in the RAF so far.

Location Map of RAF Stations and other facilities in Germany between 1955 and 1984

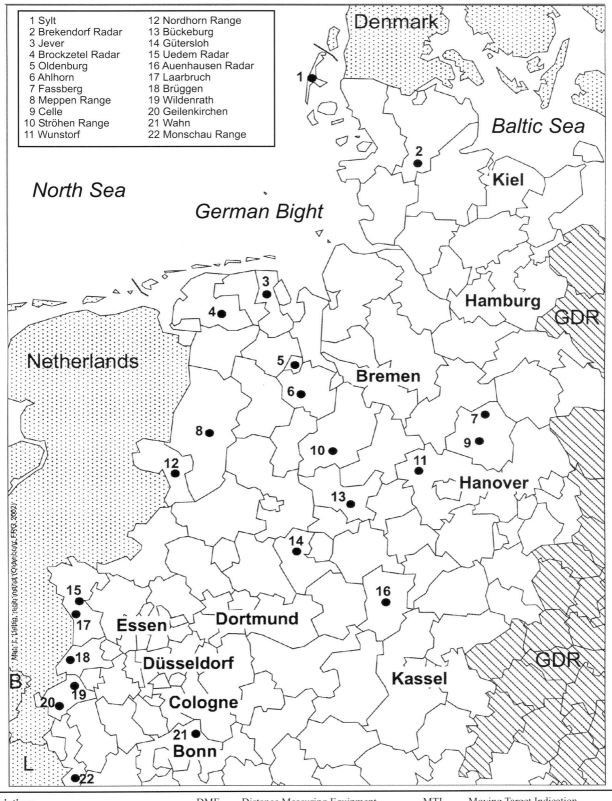

Legend:

1 Sylt
2 Brekendorf Radar
3 Jever
4 Brockzetel Radar
5 Oldenburg
6 Ahlhorn
7 Fassberg
8 Meppen Range
9 Celle
10 Ströhen Range
11 Wunstorf
12 Nordhorn Range
13 Bückeburg
14 Gütersloh
15 Uedem Radar
16 Auenhausen Radar
17 Laarbruch
18 Brüggen
19 Wildenrath
20 Geilenkirchen
21 Wahn
22 Monschau Range

Map labels: Denmark, Baltic Sea, Kiel, North Sea, German Bight, Hamburg, GDR, Netherlands, Bremen, Hanover, Essen, Dortmund, Düsseldorf, Kassel, Cologne, Bonn, GDR

Map: E. Liebig, regio institut, Oldenburg, FRG, 2002.

Abbreviations		
ADIZ	Air Defence Identification Zone	
APC	Armament Practice Camp	
APS	Armament Practice Station	
2 ATAF	Second Allied Tactical Air Force	
4 ATAF	Fourth Allied Tactical Air Force	
BAFO	British Air Forces of Occupation	
BFN	British Forces Network	
CMU	Command Maintenance Unit	
CO	Commanding Officer	
CRDF	Cathode Ray Direction Finding	
DME	Distance Measuring Equipment	
GCA	Ground-Controlled Approach	
GCI	Ground-Controlled Interception	
GDR	German Democratic Republic	
GSM	General Situation Map	
IFF	Identification Friend or Foe	
IPN	Iso-Propyl Nitrate	
Jabo	Jagdbombergeschwader (Luftwaffe Fighterbomber Wing)	
JG	Jagdgeschwader (Luftwaffe Fighter Wing)	
MTI	Moving Target Indication	
OCU	Operational Conversion Unit	
QRA	Quick Reaction Alert	
R/T	Radio/Telephone	
TACAN	Tactical Air Navigation	
2 TAF	Second Tactical Air Force (i.e. RAF)	
TTS	Target Towing Squadron	
UHF	Ultra High Frequency	
UK	United Kingdom	
VHF	Very High Frequency	
WTS	Weapons Training Squadron	

GCI Radar Stations

When the first 2TAF Hunters arrived in April 1955 the RAF was using a number of "mobile" radar stations for the control of its fighter force and the surveillance of the North West German air space. These radars were not always reliable and their effectiveness could be considerably reduced under certain atmospheric conditions. Also, as all the equipment plus controllers and technicians were above ground, their vulnerability from air attacks was obvious.

This unsatisfactory situation was greatly improved in 1956/57, when four new large long range radar stations were built. These were far from mobile though, as everything, apart from their scanners, was situated well below ground in concrete bunkers but their vulnerability was much reduced

The workplaces of the controllers in front of glimmering radar screens in a scarcely lit environment had a somewhat futuristic air about it. Luftwaffe controllers under training in some of the new radar stations, found that the presentation of the overall tactical air situation seemed to be in sharp contrast though, as in true WW 2 style young WRAFs, by means of long magnetic plotting rods, moved symbols across enormous GSMs (General Situation Maps), while officers were stragically placed on galleries, to view the ever changing general situation from above.

This form of presentation was necessary, however, as the information from neighbouring radar stations could, at that time, not to be transferred electronically by data link and a simple standing (land line) phone link had to serve for the transfer of all relevant information by word of mouth to make up the overall

Marconi T.13 height finding radar

picture of the 2TAF area on the GSMs.

The new equipment was highly praised and said to be superior to equipment used by the USAF in 4ATAF, particularly as far as definition was concerned and the only criticism referred to a certain loss of coverage near the site of the radar in, surprisingly, sunny and clear conditions, when echoes from nearby "non-flying" targets produced interference with returns from aircraft. The lack of a Moving Target Indicator (MTI) on the equipment was apparently responsible for the "problem". As the range of the new radars was such, that the areas they covered overlapped, neighbouring stations could provide the information, which, in the conditions described, the own station could not deliver.

The equipment used was Marconi Type 80 for surveillance and Marconi Type 13 for height finding. Each station had one surveillance radar and three height finding radars. This arrangement meant, that although the plan position of all targets, above a certain minimum height was always available, their relative altitude had to be measured by the separate height finding radars of which there were only three. So the altitude of only three targets could be established at one and the same time and controllers had to be very careful in the allocation of target priorities. 3 D radars which provided all relevant information of all targets only became available in the late sixties.

The locations of the four radars were at Brekendorf (south of the Danish border), Brockzetel (near the southern North Sea coast south west of Jever), Auenhausen (50 miles south west of Hanover) and Uedem (close to the Dutch border near Goch).

In the interceptor role Hunters had to use the GCI stations extensively, especially as they did not have their own

Marconi T.80 surveillance radar aerial.

search radars to guide them in the final phase of an interception. Here and on ground attack missions also the "mark one eyeball" was of vital importance. GCI stations also could be most useful in the case of other navigational aids failing as they were able, within certain limitations, to lead aircraft back to base.

In common with the Battle Flights the GCI stations were "live" continuously, 365 days a year, day and night and it was the skilful combination of the two, which made the all important early warning function so successful.

The Marconi radars in 2TAF had a long career and were only replaced from 1969, when first generation 3 D radars became available.

General Situation Map at Brockzetel GCI radar station.

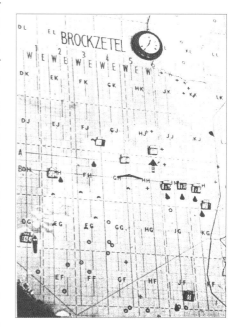

The Arrival of the Hunter

The first Hunter F.4, WW649, landed at RAF Jever on the 15 April 1955 and was earmarked for 98 Sqn. which had previously been part of 121 Wing - flying Venom FB.1s from RAF Fassberg. The other two squadrons of the wing, 118 Sqn. and 14 Sqn. were to follow in quick succession, and by June 1955, all 3 squadrons had been re-equipped with their new fighters. 118 Sqn. had joined 98 Sqn. at RAF Jever and 14 Sqn. moved to RAF Oldenburg.

The Venom FB.1 had seen a career of mixed fortunes and one of its weaker points had been its proneness to early fatigue in some areas of its wing which had led to a number of losses. No wonder therefore that its pilots had been looking forward to their new mounts. As it turned out, however, the new aircraft arrived in a low modification standard, which was not much different from that of the Hunter F.1 which had entered squadron service in Fighter Command in July 1954, so patience was of the essence before the necessary modifications could be made. As with the Hunter F.1, surging of the Avon engine at high angles of attack at altitude and during gun firing were the main problems associated with the introduction of the Hunter F.4; derating the engine eventually solved the tendency to surge at high angles of attack, while surging due to gunfire was remedied by fuel dipping, which involved the reduction of the fuel flow to the engine. As long as the original Avon 115 had not been replaced by the surge-free Avon 121 Hunter 4s were not allowed to fire high velocity ammunition above a height of 25,000 ft. - not an enviable situation for a pilot whose main task it was to intercept incoming bombers at altitudes of up to 50,000 ft.

There were more problems with the four Aden guns; in the original design of the Hunter the empty cartridge cases and belt links were ejected through chutes which ended flush with the fuselage skin. However this could cause damage to the air-brake fairing as well as to the inboard drop tanks (when carried). Tear-shaped collector tanks - called "Sabrinas" in RAF jargon, in a reference to a well-endowed British film star of the time, for the belt links, and extended chutes for a more controlled ejection of the cartridge cases were found to solve these problems.

Although the "follow-up" tailplane, a device which linked the movement of the elevators with the tailplane trim, thus achieving better longitudinal control at high Mach-numbers, was introduced on the Hunter 4, initial deliveries to the squadrons lacked this improvement and when combined with all the other shortcomings described, this understandably somewhat dampened the enthusiasm for the new aircraft. Most of the necessary modifications were carried out at the Command Maintenance Unit at RAF Bückeburg.

Hunter F.4 WW658 'O' of 98 Sqn skirts Wilhelmshaven on an early low level flight from nearby RAF Jever. Newly delivered on 20 April 1955 this aircraft has yet to be fitted with the 'Sabrina' link collectors for its Aden cannon. (MoD)

With the Venom FB.1 squadrons re-equipped it was the turn of the Sabre F.4 squadrons, starting with 26 Sqn. in June 1955 at RAF Oldenburg followed by 4 Sqn. at RAF Jever and 20 Sqn., again based at Oldenburg - all receiving Hunter 4s before the end of 1955. In January 1956 it was 93 Sqn's turn at RAF Jever and by May 1956 the "Clutch" airfields at RAF Brüggen - with 67, 71, 112 and 130 Sqns., and at RAF Geilenkirchen - with 3 and 234 Sqns., completed the re-equipment programme with Hunter F.4s.

The ex-Sabre pilots had rather mixed feelings about their new mounts, because by 1956 the Sabre was well

So new that it lacks link collectors and squadron markings F.4 WW657 is pictured in the spring of 1955 while on the strength of 118 Sqn at Jever. It carries the temporary code letter 'A' in yellow on black on the <u>inside</u> of the cockpit canopy just behind the ejection seat; in fact when fully painted in the Squadron's markings it was re-coded 'G'. (Brian Sharman)

The C.O.'s aircraft of 118 Sqn, XE665 'A' being flown by the unit's renowned aerobatics exponent, (then) Flt Lt Ken Goodwin. (MoD)

established in the squadrons and much liked by those pilots who flew it. Compared to the Hunter 4 the Sabre 4 was almost as fast in level flight, offered a superb all-round view from the cockpit and had a good endurance even without wing tanks, whereas the Hunter 4's average endurance in the interceptor role was only about 40 minutes. As Hunter 4s in 2TAF never used under-wing tanks, this unsatisfactory situation was only improved upon with the arrival of Hunter F.6s from February 1957 - but even here the overdue drop tanks only arrived several months later.

Coming back to the Sabre 4's advantages, the cockpit air-conditioning system has to be mentioned, and most importantly, its superior manoeuvrability which was partly due to its "all-flying tail", a device which linked the movement of the elevators with that of the tailplane and provided excellent longitudinal control even at high Mach numbers. The half-way house of the "follow-up" tailplane with its rather sluggish response improved the Hunter's longitudinal control but could never match that of the Sabre.

To come to a fair comparison between the two aircraft, though, one has to realise that the Hunter's primary role at the time was that of an interceptor fighter with its main task of intercepting high and fast flying bombers quickly. For this a superior rate of climb and effective armament were vital qualities, with which the Hunter was well endowed. In these respects the Hunter 4 scored well over the Sabre 4, which not only had a poorer climb rate, but also depended on external power to start its J-47 engine, which added to its inferior time to height. Furthermore, the four 30 mm Aden cannon of the Hunter were a much more effective armament against bombers than the Sabre's six 0.50 in. machine-guns, and equally importantly, the Hunter's removable gun pack, which could be pre-loaded, together with its independent engine starting system that did not rely upon ground equipment, gave it a superior turn around time between sorties. During its short career of little more than two years in 2TAF, more than 30 Sabres were lost, which seems to be a high figure for such a short period of time, and reflects to some extent, the relative inexperience of many of the pilots, combined with their youthful exuberance in flying what was then the fastest fighter in the RAF.

Despite what has been said about the disadvantages of the short endurance, it can be argued that the Hunter 4's lack of internal fuel was part of the reason for its superior climb rate and with a distance of only some 100 miles from the Iron Curtain in the case of RAF Brüggen and RAF Geilenkirchen, and much less from RAF Jever and RAF Oldenburg, this was absolutely essential. In the light of this factor, the assumption that 2TAF Hunter 4s, because of the extremely short warning times, never received drop tanks, seems to be a realistic one.

Ten Hunter 4s of 14 Sqn at Oldenburg in the autumn of 1955, revealing their early modification standard and the initial form of Squadron emblem, as displayed on the nose of the nearest aircraft in what is believed to be a blue disc. (David Parsons collection)

Hunter F.4 Operations

While the re-equipment of 13 squadrons with Hunter 4s within a period of just 15 months was nothing short of remarkable, equally impressive was the fact that the two Hunter OCUs had been able to train a sufficient number of young pilots - many of them only around twenty years of age when they joined the squadrons, and of no lesser importance was the training in parallel of ground crews at the technical schools. More senior pilots, who had already flown with operational squadrons, mainly converted to the new aircraft at squadron level; the lack of a two-seat dual-controlled Hunter trainer at this stage in the conversion process proved to be no handicap and obviously the Hunter's docile handling characteristics greatly contributed to this situation.

Due to the low modification standard of early Hunter F.4s and of ground crews having to get used to the new aircraft, serviceability was often rather poor with the consequence of fewer flying hours

per squadron than expected. Also aircraft had to go to the Command Maintenance Unit at RAF Bückeburg for various modifications such as extending the cartridge chutes of the Aden cannon and fitting belt link collectors; later modifications relating to the "follow-up" tailplane and to the Avon 115 engine were also performed at Bückeburg. It appears, though, that the learning curve as far as servicing at squadron level was concerned was quite steep, and also modifications at the CMU were of a more basic nature and did not require aircraft to be away for extended periods of time. The combined effect was a considerable improvement in serviceability and the number of flying hours steadily increased. Other modifications and equipment, such as the addition in late 1956 of Rebecca 8 (a navaid) and Green Salad (a device which enabled the pilot to home on to aircraft using electronic jamming equipment) were also progressively introduced. Another important mod. which was effected at about this time permitted all four Aden

An early delivery to 26 Sqn at Oldenburg, autumn 1955, Hunter F.4 WV268 'T' still without link collectors or extended cartridge chutes. The squadron markings are also incomplete with the Springbok's head yet to be applied to the white disc centred between the green, black, and yellow rectangles on the nose. (P.Fehlauer)

cannon to be fired simultaneously.

The monthly war exercise between No.2 Group - which comprised the northern airfields such as Jever and Oldenburg - against No.83 Group - including southern airfields such as Brüggen and Geilenkirchen - could see up to 60 aircraft airborne at one and the

Hunter F.4 WW663 'H', the aircraft chosen by the C.O. of 14 Sqn as his personal mount and therefore adorned with his rank pennant below the cockpit, photographed on the hardstanding outside the squadron hangar on 18 March 1957 and evidently to a high modification standard. Unusual among RAF Hunters is the unpainted natural metal rear fuselage, and this feature appears to be unique to a small number of 2TAF Hunter 4s in 1956/57. (Air Cdr B. B. Batt)

Delivered to 26 Sqn at Oldenburg on 13 June '55 this F.4 WV256 'D' was still in pristine condition when photographed in September sunshine that year, fully marked in its attractive squadron livery but as yet without 'Sabrinas' or extended cartridge chutes. (H.Weichardt)

same time. Pilots claimed that on those occasions, when the day fighters could take advantage of the long daylight hours of summer up to eight sorties could be flown in a day! Even when taking into account the short average sortie duration of just 40 minutes, this sounds exceptional, especially when compared to today's often miserable situation.

The all-important use of the guns, the Hunter's only armament in the interceptor role, was practised in a more disciplined way: for this purpose the squadrons detached, usually twice a year for four weeks on each occasion, to the Armament Practice Station at RAF Sylt,

Six of 26 Sqn's Hunter 4s while on detachment to the Royal Netherlands Air Force base of Eindhoven in September 1956 for the large RAF and NATO air defence exercise 'Stronghold'. Note that the nearest machine, WT778 'W' has the unusual bare metal rear fuselage. (P.Fehlauer)

which is located on one of the North Frisian Islands to the west of the Schleswig-Holstein Peninsula just south of the Danish border.

The main objective of the Armament Practice Camps was the practising of live air-to-air firing over the North Sea. The targets consisted of flags measuring twenty-four ft. by six ft. which were towed initially by Tempests, but from the autumn of 1954 by Meteor 8s. Towing speed was limited to 180 kts. and most firing took place at heights of up to 25,000 ft., although one range extended to 40,000 ft.

Before the introduction of the Hunter's ranging radar, which provided precise range information to the gyro gunsight, became available, the gunsight was manually pegged at 300 yds. Pilots would open fire when the size of the flag was three times the size of the aiming pipper. Using this method at a closing speed of some 200 kts the time available for an effective pass was only little more than a sixth of a second. The best firing angle was about 15 °s off when the flag appeared square to the attacking pilot. The ammunition used was dipped in

differently coloured paint so that hit marks on the flag could be identified after return to base and attributed to the respective individual participating pilots. Scores in the region of 25 % were considered average but under favourable conditions the best pilots managed to achieve up to 50 %. All air-to-air activities were conducted under radar control. The use of low velocity ammunition was standard at Sylt; for the use of high velocity ammunition - which was used for Battle Flight aircraft only - the gunsight had to be adjusted accordingly.

Before squadrons were due for APC at Sylt, that unit's Meteor 8 target-towing aircraft would usually deploy to their home base to give pilots the opportunity of practising their skills using their cine cameras before "going live" at Sylt. This measure was introduced to shorten the learning curve at APC and make more effective use of the time available.

Four weeks per course may seem to be a rather long time, but quite often, particularly during the winter months, poor weather conditions curtailed flying or made it impossible altogether. After

weather-imposed spells of inactivity the station, which tended to be busy even under "normal" circumstances, would teem with activity, especially during summer with long and sunny daylight hours and the maximum of four practising squadrons in residence, unusually high numbers of aircraft movements were registered. August 1958 must have been such an example in question, when according to the Operations Record Book, 6,206 aircraft movements were recorded; the highest daily total was 460 movements and the highest hourly intensity an amazing 64 movements. Seen in the light of these figures, claims that Sylt could, during such spells of highest activity, be second only to Chicago's O'Hare Airport as the busiest "airport" in the world would seem to be quite credible

Hunter T.7s only became available early in 1959, so for the Hunter F.4 squadrons several Vampire T.11s with

their two 20 mm cannon were used for weapons training and instrument rating flights etc. The Vampires did not form part of the squadrons but were attached to the station flights, and Oldenburg Station Flight for example had four T.11s on strength. Different stations made different use of the trainers: at Oldenburg they were never used for air-to-ground firing, whereas Jever did use them for this purpose, although the Jever squadrons never used their Hunter 4s for air-to-ground firing; here Hunter 4s occasionally fired their guns into the sea to give the armourers the opportunity to practice their skills under realistic conditions. The RAF at that time used three air-to-ground ranges in Germany, with squadrons normally using the ranges closest to their bases, so Brüggen and Geilenkirchen squadrons used Monschau Range near the Belgian border whereas Jever and Oldenburg used Meppen and Ströhen Ranges, both on the North German Plain.

The elegant lines of the clean Hunter F.4 are shown to perfection in this superb portrait of WV391 'Z' of 20 Sqn. (Derek Morter)

Most of the day-to-day work involved high level practice interceptions under the control of GCI radar stations. Because of the lack of external fuel the Hunter F.4 was a relatively light aircraft and due to the fact that the climb to operational height used up a considerable part of the fuel available manoeuvrability at height was quite good and a ceiling of 50,000ft could be reached and maintained without problems.

Usually air-to-air combat was between Hunters or against other RAF aircraft such as Venoms from Fassberg,

20 Sqn at Oldenburg had at least one Hunter 4 with the unpainted rear fuselage as this photograph of WV397 'B' clearly shows. (H.Weichardt)

Delivered to 98 Sqn on 12 May 1955 WT802 'P' displays the unit's scarlet red and white markings to advantage in this beautiful picture, taken before the fitment of 'Sabrina' link collectors. (Brian Sharman)

Celle and Wunstorf, Meteor NF.11s from Ahlhorn and Wahn, and Canberras from Ahlhorn and Gütersloh. Squadron exchanges allowed pilots to gain experience against aircraft types used by other NATO air forces, and for example the Canadians with their Canadair Sabre 6's frequently acted as sparring partners. The Sabre 6 with its Canadian Orenda 14

Brian Sharman, to whom we owe a huge debt for his many wonderful air-to-air photographs taken while he was a pilot with 98 Sqn where he flew Venom FB.1s before converting to Hunters. Known to his fellow pilots on the squadron as 'BB', Brian was a professional photographer for a while before he joined the RAF, and it shows! (Brian Sharman)

engine proved to be superior to the Hunter F.4 in most respects although Brüggen pilots claimed that it could be "out-turned at 25,000 ft".

With improving serviceability there was more time for slightly less important but equally enjoyable activities. Saturday mornings work often culminated in wing "balbos" in which as many aircraft as possible would indulge in formation exercises and it was not that unusual for individual squadrons to manage to have 14 aircraft airborne. The suitability of the Hunter for aerobatics is well known and it is hardly surprising that formation aerobatic teams sprung up with solo aerobatics not far behind. Across 2TAF at least five squadrons had aerobatic teams of four aircraft each practising the high art of formation skills: 93 Sqn led by Sqn Ldr Desmond Browne and from early 1957 Sqn Ldr "Paddy" Minnis and 118 Sqn led by Flt Lt Ken Goodwin - both from Jever; 20 Sqn led by Flt. Lt. Bill Gill and 26 Sqn led by Flt Lt Geoffrey Wilkinson - both from Oldenburg and last, but not least 112 Sqn with the "Skysharks" led by Flt Lt Lee Jones from Brüggen (who was destined to become leader of the Yellowjacks, the precursors of the Red Arrows).

On 1st May 1956 a competition was held at Gütersloh to select the aerobatic team and solo aerobatics display pilot to represent 2TAF at Continental air shows for that year; 93 Sqn won the team competition, while Flt. Lt. Ken Goodwin of 118 Sqn. became the solo aerobatics pilot, and thrilled many audiences throughout the season. (More detailed information on aerobatic flying is given in a later chapter).

With the closeness of the Iron Curtain a permanent state of readiness of aircraft - and especially interceptors - had to be maintained. Consequently each station had to provide a Battle Flight of two Hunters which was tasked with an immediate response to any violation of the Air Defence Identification Zone (ADIZ) along the border with the German Democratic Republic. The aircraft had to be able to scramble within 5 minutes of receiving the order; a second

pair of Hunters was kept ready to replace the first. Usually squadrons took their turn for the Battle Flight for a week at a time; most of the time when the order to scramble was received by the Battle Flight it was for practice and exercise purposes, but "live missions" included the leading back of Warsaw Pact aircraft which had strayed into West German air space, or the investigation of civil aircraft which by pilot or instrument error had deviated from their intended course.

On one occasion the scrambling of the Jever Battle Flight - on that day provided by 118 Sqn - "turned live" in a rather unexpected way: intended as a practice sortie, the target to be intercepted was another Hunter from neighbouring Oldenburg. As expected, the interception was successful and the target clearly identified. In order to document his success the 118 Sqn pilot intended to use his gun camera to have a record of the "bogey". By depressing the trigger though, not only did he operate his camera, but also fired 17 rounds of live ammunition towards his opponent. He was surprised and undoubtedly even more relieved when he realised that he had miraculously missed the Oldenburg Hunter.

It was later discovered that his gunsight had been adjusted for the use of low velocity ammunition and not the high velocity variety which he was carrying. Obviously the gun camera should have been operated by a separate switch and not the trigger. Apparently the amendment of Pilots' Notes was a consequence of this incident. It is not known whether the Oldenburg pilot realised that he was being fired at or by how narrowly he had escaped!

The arrival of the first Hunter F.6s in February 1957 for 4 Sqn at Jever foreshadowed the end of the short reign of the Hunter 4 in 2TAF day fighter squadrons. At that time it was generally anticipated that most, if not all Hunter F.4 squadrons would receive this new and more powerful variant of the Hunter. But as so often in history it was the development of a new weapon - this time the intercontinental ballistic missile -

93 Sqn's aerobatic team demonstrate their expertise with this superb classic echelon formation of Hunter F.4s led by the C.O., Sqn Ldr Desmond Browne in XE718 'A', followed by XE675 'E', XE677 'Q', and WV318 'G' during a practice sortie in 1956. WV318 was destined to have a long and varied career, later being converted to a two seat T.7, then T.7A, serving again in Germany and illustrated as such later in this book. After RAF service it was purchased privately and is currently owned by Delta Jets at Kemble who fly it regularly at air shows where it is invariably one of the highlights, in its gloss black finish. (Brian Sharman)

which led to new thinking on defence. Travelling at several times the speed of sound and armed with nuclear warheads this weapon could not be intercepted and one would hasten to add that this situation - despite ongoing attempts by the United States - has not changed to this day. Nuclear deterrence became the new key word; based on the concept of mutually assured destruction - MAD - the balance of power between the two super powers was to become the guarantor of a fragile peace for more than three decades.

This new state of affairs was bound to have a profound effect on conventional air defences by interceptor fighters and the 1957 White Paper on Defence by the British government which was published in early April took full account of the new doctrine. A much smaller fighter force would be needed, mainly for the defence of the V-bomber and missile based nuclear deterrent in the UK. In 2TAF it meant that a similarly reduced fighter force would be mainly tasked with air policing, providing air superiority over the battlefield and to an increasing extent assume ground attack tasks. The immediate effect on the Hunter 4 force was devastating: in addition to the complete Hunter wing at Brüggen the two Geilenkirchen squadrons were to go, while at Jever and Oldenburg only two squadrons survived at each base, thus

bringing the total number of Hunter F.4 squadrons to be disbanded to nine, from the original thirteen.

In the event all this happened with remarkable speed and on 10 September 1957 the last Hunter F.4 squadron, 26 Sqn at Oldenburg, was disbanded. This left just four Hunter 6 squadrons in 2TAF: Nos. 4 and 93 Sqns at Jever, and 14 and 20 Sqns at Oldenburg (moving to Ahlhorn in late September 1957 after Oldenburg had been transferred to the Luftwaffe). Interestingly both at Jever and Oldenburg the squadrons with the lower squadron numbers survived, probably due to an official policy.

Despite their short service career in 2TAF of only two and a half years, Hunter F.4s had come a long way; once the necessary modifications had been made and ground crews had acquired the

skills of maintaining the aircraft, serviceability increased dramatically and enabled the Hunter F.4 to live up to its role of the last specialised day interceptor fighter of the RAF. The aesthetic appeal of its elegant shape, uncluttered by external stores and other protuberances, are to this day unrivalled in many eyes. Sadly the sight of up to fifty Hunters, or rather the whirling criss-cross of their contrails high above, or the awesome spectacle of more than one hundred aircraft contrailing at altitude to simulate an attack by bombers on the UK, have gone for ever.

Start up! The acrid black smoke and loud hiss which accompanied the cartridge start of the Avon 115/121 powered Hunters, in this case newly delivered F.4s of 67 Sqn at Brüggen in the spring of 1956. (via Peter Caygill)

Hunter F.6 Operations

Benefiting from the elimination of the problems which had so much plagued early Hunter F.4s and the introduction of the surge-free Rolls Royce Avon 203 engine, which provided an increase in thrust of 33 %, the Hunter F.6 was the aircraft which the RAF had been waiting for.

With the new engine came the AVPIN (Plessey Isopropyl Nitrate) liquid fuel starting system to replace the cartridge starter of the Hunter 4. Apart from an improvement in general reliability it shortened the starting process and combined with the added power of the new Avon enabled the Hunter 6 to stay ahead of the American supersonic F-100 Super Sabre until a height of some 40,000 ft. was reached. Although the Super Sabre had a superior climb rate it relied on a rather slow external starter and was still on the runway when the Hunter was already climbing away.

Other refinements which improved the handling of the Hunter F.6 included the introduction of an extension of the outboard wing leading edge, which cured the tendency to a certain pitch-up. On the other hand a minor pitch-down which was encountered when the guns were fired at altitude could be remedied by fitting gun blast deflectors to the cannon ports, and the extended cartridge chutes of the Hunter F.4 were further extended on the Hunter 6. Navigation was made easier by the availability of ground stations which allowed full use of DME, and this mark also benefited from the general introduction in the RAF of UHF radio soon after this variant entered operational service.

Despite the considerable increase in power the maximum level speed of the Hunter F.6 differed little from that of earlier Hunters, mainly because of aerodynamic limitations - especially of the wings - prevented any significant improvement; a direct result of that added power, however, was improved manoeuvrability as a result of higher sustainable turning speeds. The follow-up tailplane of the Hunter 4 was retained with the consequence that the

Hunter 6 inherited rather poor longitudinal control at high Mach numbers.

After the teething troubles with the Hunter 4 some two years earlier, which were due to the low modification standard of earlier aircraft, one would have expected Hunter 6s to be modified to full standard when they reached the squadrons. Surprisingly this was not so and the initial arrivals lacked outboard wing extensions, gun blast deflectors and longer cartridge chutes. In day-to-day flying, though, this did not matter much as the modifications were of a minor nature and their temporary absence did not lead to flying restrictions as experienced with the Hunter 4.

The introduction of the bigger Avon 203 engine had led to a slight reduction of the internal fuel capacity, and although specific fuel consumption had been reduced when compared to the Avon 115 and 121 engines of the Hunter 4, the increase in thrust meant a higher consumption in absolute terms, with the combined result of an even shorter duration of the Hunter 6 than its predecessor. This of course made the use of the inboard drop tanks with a fuel capacity of 100 gallons each a definite must. Again drop tanks were not available when the aircraft arrived from the MUs in the UK and it took months before the deliveries began. However, there was a bonus, too, as pilots were able to take full advantage of the additional power of the new engine and indulge in the superior climb rate and manoeuvrability of the "clean" Hunter, which the Hunter 4 and most other fighters in NATO - at that time - were clearly not capable of. Pilots were well advised though, to always have an eye on the fuel gauge!

It is not without irony that at a time when the new Hunter F.6s in 2TAF lacked most of the refinements of the later aircraft of that mark, licence-built Dutch Hunter F.4s were flying with extended outer wing leading edges, inboard wing drop tanks and gun-blast deflectors. In the case of the Hunter 6 it was not before 1959 that all RAF aircraft had been modified to full standard. Most of the modifications were made at Laarbruch to which the CMU had moved after Bückeburg had been transferred to the German Heer.

When first issued to 14 Sqn in the spring of 1957 their factory - fresh Hunter F.6s were as yet without all the later refinements which would enhance their operational capability, and still retained the inherent elegance of the design, shown in this pleasing study of XG131 'N' on final approach to land at Oldenburg. (H. Weichardt)

(Opposite) You can almost feel the 'G' come on as this four ship of 14 Sqn Hunter F.6s execute the standard 'fighter break' on return to their home base of Ahlhorn in April 1958, preparatory to joining the circuit on the down-wind leg of the pattern. They comprise XJ644 'C', XJ673 'E', XG292 'R', and XJ646 'D', all without the extended saw-tooth leading edge wing, gun blast deflectors, or other mods which were to follow. (David Parsons collection)

To come back to the arrival of the Hunter F.6 in 2TAF, it took just four months to re-equip the four squadrons, 4 Sqn. and 93 Sqn. at Jever in February and March 1957 and 14 Sqn. and 20 Sqn. at Oldenburg in April and May 1957. With the transfer of Oldenburg to the Luftwaffe in late September 1957 the two squadrons deployed to Ahlhorn as their new base, joining 96 and 256 Sqns with Meteor NF.11s, before the Meteors moved on to Geilenkirchen in February 1958. Unexpectedly in June 1958 - and more than a year after the re-equipment of the first four squadrons - another squadron of Hunter 6s was re-formed at Ahlhorn. This was 26 Sqn which had formerly flown Hunter 4s at Oldenburg in company with 14 and 20 Sqns. until September 1957 so the wing was complete again with the three squadrons and bringing the total number of Hunter 6 squadrons in 2TAF to five.

Apparently it was the defence planners' realisation that with the disbandment of nine Hunter 4 squadrons and the remaining six Venom squadrons between April and November 1957 there was insufficient ground attack capability left in 2TAF to fulfil the RAF's NATO commitment in Germany, which led to the re-formation of 26 Sqn at Ahlhorn. In fact the addition of a fifth squadron made virtually no difference to the total number of F.6s deployed in Germany, since most of the twelve aircraft allocated to the newly reformed 26 simply came from a redistribution of those already on the

20 Sqn Hunter F.6 XJ718 'T' returning from air-to-ground firing work in August 1957. (H.Weichardt)

strength of the other four squadrons. Unit establishment had in any case steadily been reduced, from 18 or 22 aircraft per squadron during the Sabre era, to 16 or more usually 14 when 2 TAF fighter squadrons re-equipped with the Hunter F.4, and generally to only 12 aircraft from June 1958 when the four F.6 squadrons were obliged to donate aircraft to re-establish the new No. 26 Squadron. It was Ahlhorn's turn to be transferred to the Luftwaffe in September 1958, which made another move of 14, 20, and 26 Sqns necessary. This time it was to Gütersloh, their final base with Hunter 6s.

With the Hunter F.4s air defence had been the primary role and ground attack a secondary, almost negligible task; with the new defence strategy as a result of the 1957 White Paper the situation was not reversed but much more emphasis was put on air-to-ground activities. For this the Meppen and Ströhen ranges and later also Nordhorn range, close to the Dutch border, were used extensively. From early 1959 Hunter T.7 two-seaters became available and at long last weapons training could be conducted on the same type of aircraft.

Despite the new emphasis on ground attack the use of the Armament Practice Station at Sylt for live air-to-air firing went on unchanged, and Hunter 6 squadrons would deploy to Sylt twice a year for four weeks at a time. Air-to-air firing followed pretty much the same pattern as previously described for the Hunter 4. With the availability of the Hunter 6's ranging radar the rather unrealistic manual setting of the gyro gunsight at a fixed range - as on the Hunter 4s - had obviously gone, as the

radar now fed precise range information to the gunsight for automatic range setting. The reliability of the Hunter 6's ranging radar was, however, not always satisfactory and in September 1958 a very high abortive sortie rate was recorded at Sylt so that an investigation into the problem was called for.

When under-wing drop tanks were supplied to the squadrons in late 1957 it was normally just the inboard tanks that were used although most aircraft carried four pylons as standard fit. Outboard tanks were mainly used for ferry flights or for deployments to bases further afield. It was also claimed that the gain in range by the use of outboard wing tanks was marginal, as the position of the tanks in a high drag area much reduced the benefits of the additional fuel capacity.

One activity which did not require wing tanks was, of course, aerobatics and 93 Sqn's team of four which - after its success in 1956 on Hunter F.4s - again won its slot as the official aerobatics team to represent 2TAF. This time it was led by its new CO, Sqn. Ldr. "Paddy" Minnis. The competition at Gütersloh on the 1 May 1957 against 20 Sqn of Oldenburg also again brought success for Flt. Lt. Ken Goodwin of 118 Sqn as solo aerobatics pilot. He usually accompanied the team to displays all over Europe - from Helsinki to Cannes - and both thrilled audiences with their unique flying skills. Interestingly Ken Goodwin, being a member of 118, did not have a Hunter F.6 at his disposal. Forgetting traditional rivalry between the squadrons 93 Sqn had the generosity to provide him with one of their Hunter 6s which gave his already spectacular solo performance that extra sparkle. Rumour has it that members of 118 Sqn once managed to paint their black and white wavy line markings on the borrowed aircraft. If this

was so it could perhaps explain the erroneous belief that 118 Sqn received "some" Hunter 6s just before disbanding in late August 1957.

Sadly 1957 also marked the end of official solo and formation aerobatic flying in 2TAF; the Command with its much reduced size no longer seemed to justify its "own" aerobatic representation; to fill the gap the Fighter Command teams - initially the "Black Arrows" of 111 Sqn and subsequently the "Blue Diamonds" of 92 Sqn - were the highlights of many RAF air days in Germany in the late fifties and early sixties. For audiences this of course was an improvement on what 2TAF had been able to offer in the past. The appearance of the 16 specially painted Hunters of the "Blue Diamonds" at Ahlhorn in 1962 was a performance which probably has not been surpassed on the Continent to this day.

Jever's aerobatic exploits were not only followed by the local press, they also got a frequent mention in the short weekly BFN (British Forces Network) news bulletin on 2 TAF. Oldenburg's notoriety on BFN had quite a different reason. One of its units - 20 Sqn - had a most unusual mascot. "Plt. Off. Elbert Du Crossis" was a tiny tortoise which had been picked up by its keeper and trainer Fg. Off. Ralph Owen at 1 a.m. after a night out with fellow pilots in downtown Oldenburg. When they returned to their car they had found out that it had been parked right in front of a pet shop window behind which a number of tortoises were still active. The thought that one of them would make an excellent mascot for the squadron almost coincided with Fg. Off. Owen's knock on the door which unexpectedly resulted - with some understandable delay - in the emergence of a rather sleepy shop owner. The following negotiation was successful and the shop owner insisted on presenting Fg. Off. Owen with the said tortoise - free of charge. Plt. Off. Ducrossis - complete with Flying Log Book and Service Identity Card - got used to his new environment quickly. Wherever the squadron travelled he accompanied them in his box on the instrument panel on one of the Hunters as far as Cyprus. His speciality was supersonic dives and he never needed - even at 40,000ft - extra oxygen. Off-duty activities culminated in him being spoon-fed his favourite Bavarian beer on top of the bar in the Officers' Mess, when a strategic positioning of various chairs was necessary to prevent him from launching himself into space. Ducrossis - not unexpectedly - went through the ranks quickly and was promoted to Sqn Ldr within five years.

Saturday morning flying was still going on in the late fifties but the rest of the weekend was normally "free" unless exercises - quite frequently - continued right through the weekend. Urgent air tests though, would take place whenever deemed necessary. In the case of such flights taking place on Sundays pilots had a lot of air space just to themselves and occasionally saw this as a challenge to try something creative which they would not think of doing during "normal" flying. On one such occasion a Gütersloh pilot must have thought it would be a good idea to test the alertness of the radar controllers of the own side on a grey Sunday afternoon. After take-off at Gütersloh he had made sure by flying at minimum height, not be detected by radar. On an easterly heading he had

(Below) 20 Sqn's mascot 'Flying Officer Elbert Ducrossis', at that time probably the only supersonic tortoise worldwide, with (right) its 'keeper' Fg Off Ralph Owen. (Ralph Owen)

93 Sqn's aerobatic team led by new C.O. 'Paddy' Minnis with four freshly delivered Hunter 6s practising off the North Sea coast: XG294 'A', XJ632 'C', XJ676 'S', with XJ641 in the box, as yet uncoded, but soon to become 'G'. The escarbuncle squadron badge on the nose is just visible, whereas the 'golden arrow' markings which hitherto flanked the fuselage roundels on the squadron's previous F.4s have yet to be reinstated, in miniature, to the nose of the F.6s, and even then were a very poor substitute. ('Flight' via Roger Lindsay)

turned parallel with the border to the GDR and accelerated to maximum speed before climbing steeply to over 40,000 ft. and then turned on a westerly heading. Obviously RAF radar controllers were more than a little intrigued about the mysterious "arrival" on their screens - and with the IFF turned off there was no way of identifying it. So the nearest Battle Flight - it happened to be Gütersloh's - was scrambled. When eventually contact was made with the "intruder" pilots found it hard to believe that they had intercepted a fellow pilot from their own station. Although their own side had passed this test brilliantly, creative flying of this kind was not encouraged. Reactions from the other side of the border - judged by an incident in the past when an Ahlhorn-based Meteor NF. 11 had come under fire from a MiG - tended to be rather unpredictable and could potentially have lead to unwanted consequences.

One incident in the summer of 1960 - although no Hunters were involved - was widely reported in the press and led to a minor diplomatic row between Britain and Germany. Her Majesty The Queen was on a return flight from Copenhagen after a state visit in Denmark when her Comet flying at some 35,000 ft. over the German North Sea coast near Emden was used as a practice target by two Luftwaffe Sabres from the Sabre OCU at Oldenburg. It was never revealed whether the German pilots had been briefed about the presence of the Royal Flight during their sortie. Visibility was excellent on that day and the German pilots should have realised the special status of the Comet even without prior briefing; also it is not clear whether Brockzetel Radar, which controlled that area and was under RAF command at that time, might have been able to prevent the incident.

As with the Hunter F.4s, day-to-day flying included many practice encounters with other RAF aircraft and increasingly with aircraft of the new Luftwaffe. They were mainly Canadian-built Sabre 6s which the Luftwaffe used in the day fighter role and F-84 F Thunderstreak fighter bombers. The Sabre 6 had a performance which made it superior to the Hunter F.6 in some respects such as manoeuvrability at certain heights, and range. The Hunter 6 scored though, when it came to acceleration, climb rate and fire power, attributes which were vital for the interception of high flying bombers and also ground attack tasks but to a lesser extent when air superiority had to be established over a battle field against other fighters like the Sabre 6 with its superior manoeuverability. Fighter bombers such as the Thunderstreak used to fly at very low level and were difficult to detect anyway but particularly by the "radarless" Hunter. GCI radar stations were of little help either, as they, too, were unable to detect low flying aircraft.

In retrospect it is interesting to see that the cuts in RAF strength as the consequence of the 1957 White Paper on Defence were less drastic in 2TAF when put into perspective. Reductions in the numbers of Hunter day fighter squadrons and Venom fighter bomber squadrons were largely compensated by the formation of two Luftwaffe day fighter wings with Sabre 6s in 1959 - JG 71 at Ahlhorn and JG 72 at Leck just south of the Danish border. Also 3 fighter bomber wings with F- 84F Thunderstreaks had been formed from January 1958 with Jabo 31 at Nörvenich, Jabo 35 at Husum and Jabo 36 at Hopsten.

It is also worth stating that the White Paper did not call for a reduction of the night/all-weather fighter force which was kept at a level of four squadrons until 1961, when it was reduced to two squadrons of Javelins, which, however, were "assisted" by JG 71 at Wittmundhafen which had changed to the all-weather fighter role with F-104 Gs from mid-1963.

Obviously, within a more complex air defence environment and advances in relevant technologies the day fighter breed had become obsolescent. The arrival of supersonic missile-armed all-weather fighters such as the F-102, F-104 and somewhat later the Lightning, with their advanced search radars and infrared guided missiles, and in the case of the F-102 even radar guided missiles, had started a new era in air defence. It was no surprise therefore, that four of the five Hunter F.6 squadrons in RAF Germany - as it was called from 1st January 1959 - were disbanded in December 1960, leaving 14 Sqn (with unit establishment increased to about 18 fighters) to carry on for another two years until December 1962. This made 14 Sqn the longest serving Hunter day fighter squadron in the RAF, beating 92 Sqn by 6 months.

It seems fitting that it was the Hunter which marked the end of the long line of RAF day fighters; the combination of its superior performance in combat terms and unparalleled aesthetic appeal produced a unique blend which is unlikely ever to be achieved again.

Hunter 6 XE546 'M' of 26 Sqn coming in to land at its Gütersloh base in the summer of 1959, exhibits a late mod. state and carries four under wing pylons 'though typically only those inboard are fitted with 100 gal. drop tanks, and these are so far without stabilising fins. (D.Schmidt)

Hunter T.7 Service in Germany

The arrival of the Hunter trainer in Germany was rather late in the day and some four years after the Hunter 4 started to equip the first squadrons, so squadrons had to make do and conduct instrument and weapons training in Vampire T.11s, which were attached to the Station Flights of the Hunter bases. This situation remained even after the arrival of the Hunter 6 from February 1957 and lasted until early 1959 when Hunter T.7s were delivered to the Station Flights at Gütersloh, which had three Hunter 6 squadrons and Jever, which had two Hunter F.6 squadrons. Also the Armament Practice Station at Sylt acquired Hunter T.7s for weapons training with 402 Weapons Training Squadron, which displaced the Vampire T.11s previously used.

2 and 4 sqns, from 1961, in contrast to most of the Hunter squadrons in RAF Germany, each had their own T.7 and used them until disbandment as Hunter operators. Before Lightning T.4s became

available, 19 and 92 Sqns at Gütersloh and Geilenkirchen respectively, used Hunter T.7s for a short period.

Even after the last Hunter squadron had left Germany, 15 and 16 Sqns, flying Buccaneers from Laarbruch, were using T.7s and T.7As for instrument training and carried on doing so until they were disbanded in 1983 and 1984 respectively (prior to which eight additional two-seat Hunters were issued to Laarbruch Station Flight for use by these squadrons while the Buccaneers were temporarily grounded). The T.7A lacked radio Compass, gun and all provision for bombs and rockets.

Most of the Hunter trainers were new-build aircraft but a small number were converted Hunter 4s which had become available with the disbandment of most of the squadrons flying that type. With the Hunter F.4 the T.7 shared the "small" Avon engine, in this case the Avon 121a and 122, and due to the difference in performance compared with the more powerful Hunter 6, training involving the two aircraft tended

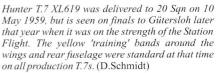

Hunter T.7 XL619 was delivered to 20 Sqn on 10 May 1959, but is seen on finals to Gütersloh later that year when it was on the strength of the Station Flight. The yellow 'training' bands around the wings and rear fuselage were standard at that time on all production T.7s. (D.Schmidt)

to lack some realism, as allowances had to be made for the performance differential, especially as far as the climb rate was concerned. Compared to the single seaters, the T.7 retained only one Aden cannon on the starboard side for its role as a weapons trainer and had provision for rocket pods. It could carry up to four 100 gal. drop tanks and had a brake parachute. Avionics included UHF radio, radio compass and TACAN for a small number of T.7A's.

The most conspicuous difference between the single and two-seat versions of the Hunter is obviously the widened front fuselage, to allow side-by-side seating. With the hood fairing blending elegantly into the dorsal spine, the elongated nose section, saw-tooth wing leading edge and extended tail cone to accommodate the brake parachute, the T.7 certainly rivals the good looks of the single seaters. Some observers even claim, that with the more refined aesthetics, it is in a class of its own.

Interestingly Hunter T.7s survived longest in RAF Germany and when the last aircraft left in 1984, a quarter of a century of service in the command had been reached. If the length and breadth of Hunter operations here is a sign of the usefulness of this superb aircraft, then there is only one rival, the unique Harrier which, not surprisingly, happens to come from the same stable.

XL621, another T.7 of the Gütersloh Station Flight at a later date by which time the yellow training bands had been superseded by large areas of fluorescent orange paint on nose, wings, and tail. (Roger Lindsay collection)

Hunter FR.10 Operations

The flexibility of the basic Hunter design was realised at an early stage and Hawker Aircraft decided as early as 1956 that fighter reconnaissance was one of the areas in which the aircraft could make a useful contribution, so Hunter F.4 WT 780 was modified by the company and its standard nose section, containing the ranging radar, was replaced by a five-camera nose. This was a private project and as such did not receive any government funding and at that time the RAF remained undecided as to whether the project deserved any support.

Apparently the Swift FR.5, the Hunter FR.10's predecessor, was never intended to be more than a stop gap, before, eventually, reconnaissance Hunters became available. The rather short range of the Swift and its increasingly difficult serviceability situation most likely convinced the RAF that a replacement would be needed sooner rather than later. Whether the idea, to convert Hunter F.4s as reconnaissance fighters was ever contemplated, is not known. The fact remains, that considerable numbers of this mark of Hunter were withdrawn from RAF service in 1957, partly as a consequence of re-equipment of the squadrons with Hunter F.6s and even more so as a result of the Defence White Paper of that year; despite low flying hours, after only some two years of service, many of these aircraft were simply scrapped.

In the event the RAF decided, by utilising much of the experience gained with Hunter F.4 WT 780, in favour of a three-camera trial installation, which was tested on Hunter F.6 XF 429 and first flown in November 1958. The eventual FR.10 of which deliveries to 4 Sqn at Gütersloh started in January 1961 and to 2 Sqn at Jever in March 1961, incorporated, apart from the camera nose, features such as a brake

Hunter FR.10 XE556 'W' 2 Sqn. somewhere over the North German Plain, circa 1968 (RAF Gütersloh)

parachute, the capability of carrying 230 gal. drop tanks on the inner wing pylons, UHF radio and a radio compass. Also Avon 207 engines, basically late standard Avon 203s as used on the Hunter F.6, were used. Gun blast deflectors were no longer needed as the aircraft was to be used mainly in low level operations. Finally the addition of armour plating under the cockpit floor was a useful means of protecting pilots, particularly during low level operations.

Most of these features of the FR.10 were shared with the FGA.9 version of the Hunter which was never based in RAF Germany. Also the FR.10 and FGA.9 shared their common descent from the Hunter 6 in that both were conversions of this aircraft and neither of them newly built. When the first of 32 Hunter FR.10s was delivered to RAF Gütersloh on 5th January 1961, it went to 4 Sqn which had flown Hunter F.4s and F.6s from Jever until their disbandment on 30 December 1960 on

which date 79 Sqn, with Swift FR.5s at Gütersloh, had been re-numbered 4 Sqn.

As could be expected, the Hunter was now a mature aircraft and its serviceability far superior to its predecessor, while in terms of range, with the ability to carry 230 gal. drop tanks in addition to the 100 gal. drop tanks, it also scored over the Swift.

In contrast to the day fighter Hunters the primary task of the Hunter FR.10 was photo-reconnaissance. As the powerful 30 mm Aden cannon had been retained, a secondary ground-attack capability, mainly to be used on opportunity targets and the ability to defend itself, came in handy. The camera nose of the FR.10 housed three Vinten F.95 oblique cameras with lenses of 4 or 12 inch focal length for 70mm film in interchangeable film magazines for 500 exposures. To allow photography at very high speeds and low level, exposure times of up to 1/2000 second could be used at a cycle rate of 4 to 8 frames per second.

The cameras were protected by hydraulically operated shutters which opened automatically when the cameras were triggered. A thermostatically controlled heating element ensured that the system could operate between - 20 and + 50 degrees C. There was no "viewfinder" in the cockpit but pilots

The business end of Hunter FR.10s 'C' and 'G' of 4 Sqn at Gütersloh in September 1961, when the aircraft still have silver under surfaces and lack the yellow 'Rescue' arrow left of the canopy emergency release of later years. The significance of the 'square' left of the cannon port is unknown. (A.Saal)

Crisp echelon formation by a quartet of Hunter FR.10s of 4 Sqn circa 1967, from left to right comprising XJ714 'B', 'E' (probably XF436), 'G' (probably WW593), and XF580 'D'; note that only 'B' and 'D' have white serial numbers. (RAF Germany)

quickly gained experience of positioning their aircraft in ways which allowed the cameras to achieve the required cover. Newcomers to the recce. business would scribe marks in chinagraph pencil on their cockpit canopies as an aiming device before they learned to use the cameras more instinctively.

Photography and visual reconnaissance worked together and the Hunter FR.10 had the advantage of having a voice recorder in the cockpit, the use of which reduced the workload on the pilot, who was no longer required to take notes on his knee pad while flying at 500 kts at very low level.

The processing of films took place in purpose-built Mobile Field Processing Units (MFPUs), where prints could be processed within 10 minutes. The photographic interpreters would use both photographs and in-flight reports (IFREPs) on which pilots elaborated after a sortie. Visual sightings were also, in case of particular urgency, reported back to the ground by means of radio. This method of communication was not always without problems, as the low level range of the UHF radio could be -very limited, depending on the nature of terrain and also due to the possibility of jamming and listening in to uncoded messages. The main customer of the "products" which the reconnaissance squadrons provided, was of course the Army, and their Ground Liaison Officers (GLOs) were the link between the two.

The four 30 mm Aden cannon of the Hunter FR.10 and their usefulness for ground attack and self defence was practised throughout their career in Germany; initially the Sylt air-to-air range was used and from 1962, after Sylt had been transferred to the Luftwaffe, air-to-air firing was practised off the Dutch coast, when the Hunters operated from RNAF Leeuwarden, while the Terschelling range nearby was ideal for air-to-ground work. The use of the cannon on ground targets took place right across the Continent, depending on where a detachment would lead a squadron. Ströhen and Meppen ranges and after they were closed, Nordhorn range, were, because of their closeness to Gütersloh, extensively used. The success of the Hunter FR.10 in the low-level reconnaissance role, which was proven again and again and not least by coming out on top in numerous exercises and competitions against formidable opponents, such as the RF-4C, RF-101 Voodoo and RF-104G at the prestigious Royal Flush and Big Click events, was due, as in many success stories, to a variety of factors. To start with, the aircraft itself with its superb F.95 cameras, manoeuvrability, range and last but not least reliability, provided the foundation. Combined with the typical training approach of the RAF, with its emphasis on realistic conditions, which included pilots, processing and interpretation specialists, and not least the servicing crews to keep the aircraft going, produced a mix which was difficult to beat. Other teams would excel in certain areas but rarely was there a combination of factors which proved to be so successful as the Hunter FR.10, the last dedicated reconnaissance fighter of the RAF.

Hunter FR.10 XE605 'O' just after take-off from Gütersloh (Günther Kipp)

Groups, Wings, Squadrons and Stations

In the mid-fifties, when the overall strength of 2TAF was some 35 squadrons, the Command was sub-divided into groups, wings and squadrons. 2 Group with headquarters at Sundern near Gütersloh controlled the northern airfields such as the Hunter stations of Jever, Oldenburg, Ahlhorn and Gütersloh. 83 Group with headquarters at Wahn near Cologne controlled the southern airfields such as Brüggen and Geilenkirchen. Wings were usually tied to a certain station to control the squadrons based there with a Wing Leader in the rank of a Wing Commander in charge of all flying activities. When squadrons moved to another station they came under the control of the Wing based at that station.

In 2 Group 122 Wing at Jever controlled 4, 93, 98 and 118 Sqns and from 1957 also 2 Sqn. 124 Wing at Oldenburg controlled 14, 20 and 26 Sqns. After 14 and 20 Sqns moved to Ahlhorn they came under the control, with the resident 96 and 256 Sqns, of 125 Wing of which 26 Sqn also became part, after it reformed there in 1958. When Ahlhorn eventually transferred to the new Luftwaffe, 14, 20 and 26 Sqn moved to Gütersloh where they, together with 79 Sqn, were controlled by 121 Wing.

In 83 Group 135 Wing at Brüggen controlled 67, 71, 112 and 130 Sqns whereas 138 Wing at Geilenkirchen controlled 3 and 234 Sqns, and until October 1957, No 2 Sqn.

Often Wing Leaders would have their "own" aircraft which frequently wore special markings. Servicing of these aircraft was usually the job of Station Flights rather than that of one of the squadrons of the Wing.

With the run-down of 2TAF and its re-naming as RAF Germany on 1st January 1959 came the disbandment of 2 Group in November 1958 and 83 Group in June 1958. Obviously the much

(Above) A four ship formation of 118 Sqn F.4s, led by Flt LT Ken Goodwin as they climb towards the top of a loop, comprising WT743 'R', XE682 'Z', with 'G', and 'S'. (Brian Sharman)

reduced size of the Command did not justify the existence of Groups. The Wings fared little better. The Oldenburg and Ahlhorn wings had been disbanded when their airfields transferred to the Luftwaffe in 1957 and 1958 respectively. For the surviving wings the end came in January 1960.

Even after this date it was quite common to refer to the squadrons based at a particular station as the "Gütersloh Wing" although these "Wings" did not have a formal identity with a wing number and wing leader.

(Below) Representative aircraft of 122 Wing at Jever in 1958 in front of Flying Wing Headquarters which also housed Air Traffic Control, the 'tower' is visible just above the fin of the Swift, with three servicemen in front of it. Aircraft are Hunter F.6 XG294 'A' of 93 Sqn, Swift FR.5 'S' of 2 Sqn (with PRU Blue under surfaces), and Hunter 6 XG269 'W' of 4 Sqn. (W.Zucht)

Stations, Wings and Squadrons
2 Group

RAF Jever - 122 Wing

RAF Jever, an ex-Luftwaffe airfield built in 1935/36, was used by the RAF from 1952 after it had received a concrete runway and taxiways for jet operations. In common with many other RAF day fighter stations its initial equipment had been Vampires, followed by Sabres, when in April 1955 the first Hunter 4s arrived. Hunters of various marks were flown until September 1961 and the airfield was transferred to the new Luftwaffe in December 1961.

2 Squadron

On 1 January 1961 the first pair of five Hunter F.6s were received by 2 Sqn purely as an interim measure to assist in the conversion process from Swift FR.5s to the new Hunter FR.10s which were to replace them and become the standard equipment for the squadron until March 1971, when they were displaced by Phantoms. The last of the F.6s departed on 21 March 1961 by which time enough FR.10s had been delivered to enable the full re-equipment to be completed, and although the squadron had one of the longest careers on Hunters in Germany, its time at Jever was very short indeed, because it moved to Gütersloh on 9 September 1961.

4 Squadron

The longest serving operational Hunter squadron, not only in 2TAF but in the RAF as a whole, started its association with the aircraft when it received Hunter F.4s in July 1955, which were replaced by Hunter F.6s in February 1957, and used until 30 December 1960 when the squadron was disbanded. However, 4 Sqn was in business again the very next day when 79 Sqn, flying Swift FR.5s at Gütersloh was re-numbered 4, and re-equipped with Hunter FR.10s

93 Squadron

The last of the Jever squadrons to receive Hunter F.4s in January 1956.

After little more than a year these gave way to Hunter 6s in March 1957. This mark was used right through to 31 December 1960, when the squadron disbanded.

98 Squadron

This squadron marked the beginning of the Hunter era in 2TAF when its first Hunter F.4 arrived at Jever on 15 April 1955. Alas, its career was to be short as it fell victim to the 1957 White Paper on Defence and disbanded on 15 July 1957.

118 Squadron

The second Jever squadron which received Hunter F.4s in May 1955. It was similarly short-lived and its disbandment came on 22 August 1957, sharing the fate of 98 Sqn.

RAF Oldenburg - 124 Wing

Another ex-Luftwaffe airfield built in 1935/36, was taken over by the RAF in 1951/52 to be prepared for jet operations. Similar to Jever, Vampires and Sabres preceded the Hunter 4s, which arrived in July 1955. Oldenburg "managed" to have two squadrons re-equipped with Hunter 6s before it was transferred to the new Luftwaffe in September 1957 with its squadrons moving to nearby Ahlhorn.

14 Squadron

Destined to become the longest

Serenely cruising high above the North Sea is Hunter 4 WW650 'F' of 98 Sqn photographed in 1956. This Blackpool-built aircraft was one of two which were subsequently issued to 222 Sqn at Leuchars in March '57 from 98. (Brian Sharman)

serving Hunter day fighter squadron in the RAF, 14 Sqn received its first Hunter F.4 on 13 May 1955. Hunter F.6s followed in April 1957 and the squadron moved to its new base at Ahlhorn in September of the same year.

20 Squadron

This squadron was to be the last to receive Hunter F.4s at Oldenburg with its first aircraft arriving on 23 November 1955, although it was not until 8 December that Hunter flying began, when fifteen of 20's pilots were able to fly the new type, thanks to 14 and 26 Sqns lending some of their aircraft. After acquiring Hunter F.6s in May 1957 it made the move to Ahlhorn beginning on 23 September when ten of its aircraft took up residence there, with the transfer being completed three days later.

26 Squadron

The second Hunter F.4 squadron at Oldenburg received its first aircraft on 8 June 1955. Hunter 4s were used

118 Sqn's pilots wearing their hats the 'aerodynamic' way, aboard F.4 WW657 'G'. (Brian Sharman)

Pilots of 26 Sqn pose with Hunter 4 WV270 'Z' in front of the squadron hangar at Oldenburg. Left to Right those on the aircraft are: Fg Off Ken Lovett, Fg Off Chris Cowper, Fg Off Nigel Walpole, Flt Lt John Crowley, Fg Off John Merry, Fg Off Pogo Welch, Fg Off Alan Pollock, Fg Off Ernie Jones, Sgt Fred LeGrys, Fg Off Fred Daley; Standing, L. to R. are Flt Lt Tony Carver, Flt Lt Bob Snare, Fg Off Bill Bailey (on ladder), Fg Off Jock Waters, Flt Lt Pete Perry, Flt Lt Tony Funnell, Fg Off Jim Hawkins, Fg Off Doug Wyley, and Sqn Ldr John Severne (C.O.). (Nigel Walpole collection)

throughout its time at Oldenburg which came to an end when it was disbanded as a consequence of the 1957 White Paper on 10 September of that year.

RAF Ahlhorn - 125 Wing

Ahlhorn's history dates back to the First World War when it was used for airship operations. Similar to Jever and Oldenburg the RAF acquired the airfield in its post Korean War expansion programme in the early fifties. It opened in 1952 and was used initially by Meteor night fighters and from 1954 also Canberras. When the Hunter F.6s arrived from neighbouring Oldenburg in September 1957, they served alongside the two Meteor squadrons until February 1958 when the night fighters re-located to Geilenkirchen. When the last disbanded Oldenburg Hunter 4 squadron reformed here in June 1958, the wing regained its original strength of three squadrons. The transfer of Ahlhorn to the new Luftwaffe took place in September 1958 when the Hunter squadrons had to move again, this time to Gütersloh.

14 Squadron

After its move from Oldenburg in September 1957 14 Sqn's stay a Ahlhorn did not last very long. As the successive transfer of RAF bases to the Luftwaffe was gaining pace, it was Ahlhorn's turn in September 1958 which saw the squadron move down to Gütersloh, its final Hunter base.

20 Squadron

In parallel, 20 Sqn suffered the same fate and found itself, after only a year at Ahlhorn, on the move to Gütersloh, also in September 1958.

Hunter F.6 XG291 'O' of 14 Sqn at Ahlhorn in February 1958 with 22 pilots all over the aircraft, among them the C.O. Sqn Ldr K.E. Richardson in the air intake and Fg Off B. B. Batt sixth from the right on top of the wing. Note the inboard wing drop tank (as yet without fins), but the absence of all later mods. A complement of 22 pilots seems unusual for that time and raises the question as to whether the number of aircraft had been increased from 14 to compensate for the drastic reduction in 2TAF Hunter squadrons in 1957. (Air Cdr B.B.Batt)

After moving from Ahlhorn to Gütersloh, Hunter 6s shared the base with Swift FR.5s of 79 Sqn, two of which are seen here sandwiching Hunter 6s 'M' of 14 Sqn and 'F' of 26 Sqn. The fourth unit of 121 Wing, Gütersloh, 20 Sqn is unrepresented. Note that the nearest Swift has PR Blue under surfaces while the farthest, 'S', has silver. (MoD)

26 Squadron

The destiny of 26 Sqn as a Hunter operator in Germany is rather unique, as its disbandment with Hunter 4s at Oldenburg in September 1957, unexpectedly, was not the end of the story. Phoenix-like, it was reformed at Ahlhorn on 7 June 1958 with Hunter F.6s and so acquired a new lease of life, in the course of which it also achieved reunification of the old Oldenburg Wing with 14, 20 and 26 Sqns as part of which it moved to Gütersloh in September 1958.

RAF Gütersloh - 121 Wing

Like Jever and Oldenburg, Gütersloh was one of the new 1930s Luftwaffe airfields. As opposed to those stations though, the RAF started using it almost immediately after the end of the war from November 1945. The long list of aircraft which were stationed at Gütersloh, before the Hunters arrived in August/September 1958, include Mosquitos, Tempests, Spitfires, Vampires, Meteors, Canberras and Swifts. Together with Brüggen & Laarbruch Gütersloh was to become the longest serving RAF station in Germany.

In terms of Hunter operations Gütersloh also scored, as the station with the longest continuous association with operational Hunters not only in Germany but also in the RAF. Although Hunters only arrived in August/September 1958, it was the home to operational Hunter squadrons until March 1971.

14 Squadron

The arrival from Ahlhorn on the 15 September 1958 at Gütersloh marked the beginning of the final phase as a day fighter squadron, which was to last until 17 December 1962 and was only interrupted by a short spell at Jever from March to September 1961 when Gütersloh's runway was under repair. Thus the squadron achieved the honour of not only being the last Hunter F.6 squadron in RAF Germany but also by becoming the longest serving Hunter day fighter squadron in the RAF.

20 Squadron

The squadron was the first one to move from Ahlhorn to Gütersloh, officially on 30 August 1958, though the advance party had arrived two days earlier, with the first sorties being flown from the new base on 1 September. In February 1960 the squadron was notified that it would be disbanded at the end of the year and so it proved, with the last sorties being flown on 29 December prior to disbandment the next day.

26 Squadron

The third Ahlhorn squadron moved to Gütersloh on 8 September 1958. While the other Hunter F.6 squadrons had retained or even reduced the size of their markings inherited from their Hunter F.4 predecessors, 26 Sqn had managed to do the opposite, maybe as a compensation for their late arrival as a Hunter 6 squadron. All that flamboyance did not help much, though, and disbandment inevitably also came on 30 December 1960.

Although 121 Wing had been disbanded early in1960, the two Hunter FR.10 squadrons were destined to become long-term residents at Gütersloh:

2 Squadron

When Jever was transferred to the

93 Sqn's Hunter 6s and Swifts of 2 Sqn on a late afternoon in early spring 1960 in front of their hangars at Jever. The newly acquired yellow wing tips of 93 are just discernible on the second Hunter from the left, while in the background a 'dayglow' embellished Hunter T.7 has just touched down on the wet runway. (Wg Cdr J. B. Thornton)

new Luftwaffe, 2 Sqn's next home was Gütersloh, where it arrived on 9 September 1961. As one of the two fighter reconnaissance squadrons in RAF Germany it surpassed even the longest serving Hunter day fighter squadrons in the Command and eventually became the last squadron to operate the Hunter in Germany. When its Hunter FR.10s left Gütersloh in March 1971 the squadron had been using the type for just over ten years.

4 Squadron

When the squadron disbanded with Hunter 6s on 30 December 1960 at Jever it was reformed on the same day at Gütersloh as a fighter reconnaissance squadron with Hunter FR.10s by renumbering 79 Sqn. In the process of re-equipment with the new aircraft Hunters and Swifts operated side-by-side for about three months and the Swifts were adorned with 4 Sqn. markings on the nose while retaining their 79 Sqn markings on the rear fuselage. While Gütersloh's runway was under repair from March to September 1961 the squadron deployed to Jever. For the rest of its Hunter career in Germany it stayed at Gütersloh. When it was disbanded there as a fighter reconnaissance squadron on 30 March 1970 (although its FR.10s continued to be flown until May), it had achieved the unique status of having been equipped with Hunters for a longer period than any other operational Hunter squadron in the RAF.

83 Group
RAF Brüggen - 135 Wing

Being one of the "Clutch" bases near the Dutch border, newly built Brüggen opened in July 1953. When the first Hunter F.4s arrived in January 1956, the station was still the home to four Sabre squadrons, which had succeeded the Vampires, the first occupants of the brand-new airfield. Re-equipment with Hunter 4s was rather rapid and by May of that year the four squadrons were flying their new aircraft. The effect of the 1957 White Paper hit Brüggen most severely and it lost all its Hunter squadrons after little more than a year's service. Sadly not one of them ever managed to reform as a "flying unit" and only two were revived, temporarily, as missile squadrons.

67 Squadron

The first Brüggen squadron to receive Hunter F.4s welcomed its first aircraft on 12 January 1956. Although the general standard of modification of the Brüggen squadrons and also those of Geilenkirchen was much better than that on the first-equipped Jever and Oldenburg wings, they were not able to enjoy that advantage for long. The squadron disbanded on 31 May 1957, by which time almost every Hunter had left Brüggen.

71 Squadron

Not long after the arrival of its first Hunter F.4 on 25 April 1956 the squadron quickly reached its full strength. Although also benefiting from the advantages of the later standard of modification, less attention was obviously paid to the fact of the

alarmingly short duration of the Hunter F.4, because unsurprisingly on three separate occasions within four weeks pilots of the squadron had to land at the Dutch airfield of Volkel, with almost empty tanks. Despite its short life, the squadron had its two APCs at Sylt before it disbanded on 31 May 1957.

112 Squadron

The famous sharks received their

(Above) Flight line of eight Hunter 6s of 4 Sqn in the late winter of '59; note the CPN 4/11 GCA radar in the background. (the late Dick Millward)

(Below) XE672 'B', a Hunter 4 of 112 Sqn being refuelled at Brüggen in August 1956. (Robin Brown)

(Bottom) Seen at RNAS Abbotsinch in August 1961 after acquisition by the Royal Navy, Hunter F.4 XE689 is still resplendent in its original markings as 'K' of 234 Sqn. (Roger Lindsay)

Early arrivals with 3 Sqn and still without unit markings are Hunter 4s XF972 (later 'V'), and XF948 (later 'J') flown by (then) Fg Off D. Lavender and Fg Off Wood on 9 August '56. When used for the squadron Christmas card the picture was deliberately printed the wrong way round for aesthetic reasons, but sharp eyed rivals soon noticed that the aircraft numbers were back to front, and suggested that 3 Sqn was flying backwards for Christmas, a parody of a song by popular comedians, the Goons, entitled 'I'm walking backwards for Christmas'! (Danny Lavender)

first Hunter F.4s on 6 April 1956 and were quick to form an aerobatics team called the "Skysharks". Despite many reports of poor serviceability throughout their Hunter time, pilots were in good spirits and scored well at the August APC at Sylt. The Skysharks started practising early in 1957 in order to participate in the Command aerobatics competition in May at Gütersloh. Alas, disbandment on 31 May 1957 put an end to their ambitious plans and 112 Sqn's last Hunter left Brüggen on 21 June 1957.

130 Squadron

Here the first Hunter F.4, XE680 soon

Hunter F.4 XE689 'K' of 234 Sqn while on detachment to Sylt for APC revealing the red code letter on the nose wheel door. (Ray Sturtivant)

Pilots of 234 Sqn. in front of Hunter 4 XF991 'A' the personal aircraft of the C.O., at Geilenkirchen in May 1957 just proir to disbandment. Seated l. to r: Flt Lt Bill Watford ('A'Flt Cdr), Sqn Ldr Ted Riseley (O.C.), Flt Lt Geoff Bradford ('B'Flt Cdr). Standing left ('A'Flt), l, to r: back row: Fg Off Tim King, Fg Off Bill Hobson, Fg Off Grant Waters (Adjutant), and Fg Off George Goatham, front row Fg Off Wally Foster and Flt Lt Peter Underdown (Deputy Fly Cdr). Standing right ('B'Flt) back row: Fg Off Derek Gathercole, Fg Off John Cray, Fg Off Jac O'Dowd, Fg Off Clive Haggett, front row: Flt Lt Chris Taylor (Deputy Flt Cdr), Fg Off Dave Gleen, Fg Off Dennis Mayoux. (Bill Toozs-Hobson)

The pilots of 20 Sqn pose with their Hunter 6s and personal transport at RAF Ahlhorn in April 1958. (Chris Wilmot)

to be coded Y, arrived on 21 March 1956. The activities of the squadron were very much in line with those of the other Brüggen squadrons, but unfortunately that was also the case with its premature disbandment on 31 May 1957. The squadron had become non-operational on 30 April and the departure of their last Hunter took place on 21 May 1957.

RAF Geilenkirchen - 138 Wing

The other "Clutch" base flying Hunters was of course Geilenkirchen. After opening in May 1953 and skipping the Vampire phase, it started with Sabres and by January 1954 had two squadrons in residence. The first Hunter 4 arrived on 13 April 1956 and two squadrons were established by June 1956. With Brüggen it shared its destiny of losing all its Hunter squadrons within about a year and by the middle of July 1957 all its Hunters had left, so at this point in time 83 Group had lost all its day fighters while the surviving four Hunter 6 squadrons were based at the 2 Group airfields of Jever and Oldenburg.

3 Squadron

The squadron, being the last to receive Hunter F.4s, acquired its first aircraft on 6 June 1956. Working up with the new fighters was quite rapid and on 10 August it achieved 40 sorties with eight aircraft. It seemed to differ from other Hunter 4 squadrons by flying a relatively high number of low level cross-country sorties, a generally more unusual activity for day interceptors but probably foreshadowing the increasing use of Hunters for ground attack duties. Shortly before disbanding on 15 June 1957 it flew its highest number of sorties with 52 on 21 May 1957, a remarkable achievement so close to its last day as an operational Hunter squadron, reflecting the determination of the C.O. to give his pilots the maximum opportunity to fly this fine and exhilarating fighter aircraft, and equally importantly, maintain a high level of morale in spite of the intense disappointment which inevitably accompanied the run down of squadrons.

234 Squadron

The first Hunter F.4, XE674, arrived on 13 April 1956, and the squadron was to be the last of the "Clutch" bases' squadrons to disband which took place on 15 July 1957, although its last Hunter did not leave Geilenkichen until August.

So the short existence of six day fighter squadrons, whose main task had been the defence of the Ruhr area, had come to an untimely end. It might have come as some small consolation that the night fighter element of 2 Group, consisting of two squadrons of Meteors at Ahlhorn, was based at Geilenkirchen from February 1958 to give back some credibility to the air defence of that part of Germany.

Swansong of the RAF day fighter in Germany; 14 Sqn with 16 Hunters, pilots, and the very important ground crews on a gloomy day at its Gütersloh base shortly before disbanding on 17 December 1962. The number of aircraft on the squadron had been increased to 18 after 20 and 26 Sqns disbanded in December 1960 after which 14 Sqn became the sole surviving day fighter unit. (Derek Morter)

Camouflage and Squadron Markings

Camouflage

The Hunter F.4s and F.6s issued to the squadrons based in Germany were finished in the prevailing day fighter camouflage scheme conforming to British Standard 381 colours, comprising upper surfaces in Dark Sea Grey 638, over which a specific disruptive pattern of Dark Green 641 was applied, while under surfaces were in High Speed Silver. All these colours were in a gloss finish when new but after comparatively brief exposure to everyday squadron service they dulled to a semi-gloss condition.

The only deviation to these colours relate to a small number of F.4s that were re-finished while in service in Germany, with PRU Blue 636 under surfaces replacing the original Silver. In the absence of colour photographs such revisions are difficult to substantiate, but the monochrome illustration of XF368 'C' of 3 Squadron in this publication seems to confirm that this was one of those aircraft with PRU Blue under surfaces, and others in this scheme were reported in service with 118 Squadron.

Given that immediately prior to the entry into service of the Hunter F.4 in Germany, PRU Blue had been the standard lower surface finish on its predecessors in the form of the Vampire FB.5s, 9s, Venoms, Meteor FR.9s, PR.10s, and Sabres of 2 TAF, and later some Swift FR.5s, then it is reasonable to suppose that stocks of this colour paint would be abundant at RAF fighter bases in Germany, and at the Bückeburg CMU, and could therefore easily have been applied to a few Hunters.

Another unusual, but more widespread phenomenon was the removal of camouflage from the rear fuselage of some Hunter 4s. This was approximately at the position of frame 61 aft of the fin, and extended diagonally forward and downwards. Although apparently mainly restricted to relatively few F.4s at Oldenburg (14, 20, and 26 Sqns.), and at Brüggen (e.g. 130 Sqn), this feature was also to be found on Dutch and Belgian-built F.4s and F.6s. It has been suggested that some of the F.4s issued to German-based units had a problem with high frequency vibration in the rear fuselage which could cause metal fatigue cracks in the structure, and this area may have been stripped of paint to facilitate easier regular inspection by the engineers. It may also have involved the replacement of that part of the rear fuselage, because this phenomenon was observed mostly during late 1956 / early 1957.

Some German-based squadrons, including Nos.2, 4(FR), 67,71, and 234, painted the gun ports of their Hunters in gloss black, which made them smarter in appearance, and also easier to clean after gun-firing.

Several Hunter squadrons also painted the wingtips of their aircraft white or yellow; while this may have enhanced appearance the prime purpose was to improve conspicuity when the (monochrome) cine gun camera films were analysed.

Hunter T.7 WV372 'R' of 2 Sqn after take-off from Gütersloh, circa 1969/70. Note that the serial number beneath the starboard wing is incorrectly painted as WV327. (Günther Kipp)

(Centre Right) FR.10 XF457 'T' of 2 Sqn banking somewhere over the typical terrain of the North German Plain. (MoD)

(Right) The same aircraft, XF457 'T' of 2 Sqn in September 1970 exhibiting an early attempt at 'toning down' long before the so-called B-style roundels, without the white ring, were officially introduced. The experimental roundel returned to its original red white and blue colours after little more than a month. (E. Westersotebier)

Hunter FR.10s operated by the German-based 2 and 4 Squadrons initially wore the same Dark Sea Grey, Dark Green, Silver colours as the F.4s and F.6s, but from 1965/66 the under surfaces were progressively changed to Light Aircraft Grey 627 in line with new standards applicable throughout the RAF for aircraft in this category. Uniquely, towards the end of the FR.10's service in Germany, a single example, XF457 of 2 Squadron, was experimentally finished with non-standard roundels and fin flash from which the white elements were removed; after barely a month these reverted to red, white, and blue insignia, and therefore the accompanying photograph is quite rare.

The Hunter T.7s that were first issued to RAF units in Germany were originally delivered in the then-standard training aircraft scheme of overall Silver with 'training' bands around wings and rear fuselage in Golden Yellow 356. However, one or two aircraft in service at Sylt and with Station Flights subsequently discarded the yellow bands in favour of areas of fluorescent orange 'dayglow' paint which was then becoming in vogue, (this in turn was sometimes replaced with strips of fluorescent red self-adhesive material), applied to the nose, tail, and outer wings, during 1960/61. Soon afterwards, with the demise of Sylt and the F.6 units, the two Hunter FR.10 squadrons became the principal T.7 operators in Germany for a while, and in each case they adopted the same camouflage scheme for these two seat trainers as their FR.10s. Later, with the arrival of Lightning and Buccaneer squadrons in RAF Germany came additional examples of Hunter T.7s for instrument rating, training, and communications duties; these aircraft were finished in a wide variety of schemes mostly reflecting the current training and operational needs of the period, although there were several notable exceptions, some of which are illustrated. Similarly, the four F.6s briefly assigned to Laarbruch Station Flight in the 1980s together with some additional T.7s, while the Buccaneers were reportedly temporarily grounded, were reportedly finished in the Light Aircraft Grey, White, and Red scheme which then represented the standard training colours.

Squadron Markings and Unit Code Letters

There follows a concise summary of the main markings applicable to the RAF fighter and fighter reconnaissance Hunter squadrons in Germany; however it must be realised that there were often variations to these, especially between individual aircraft within a squadron, and over time, and this was particularly true of individual aircraft code letters. Mention should also be made of those brief instances where aircraft sometimes received unauthorised 'decorations' as a result of the attention from rival squadrons' personnel, usually when landing away from their home base, and one or two illustrations have been included to exemplify this expression of squadron 'one-upmanship'.

2 Squadron
Markings, FR.10s & T.7s:

Comprised black rectangles within which was a single white triangle, placed on each side of the fuselage roundel, and

Hunter FR.10 XE580 'D' of 4 Sqn just after take-off from Gütersloh early in 1970 (Günther Kipp)

raised above the centreline. In the mid-1960s a small Squadron badge was applied to the nose beneath the windscreen, often with the pilot's name above it, in white capital letters, sometimes on a black background stripe. This practice of displaying pilots' names was later discontinued. Aircraft serial numbers on the rear fuselage were changed from black to white, and then often reverted to black during the 10 years in which 2 Squadron operated FR.10s. It is not known whether the five F.6s that were used as interim equipment during the conversion to FR.10s carried any markings, or if they retained the insignia of their previous operators, namely 4 and 93 Squadrons.

Code Letters

Initially the code letter was simply white, above and behind the fin flash,

This shot of a Hunter F.6 of 4 Sqn at Jever shows the markings in more detail, together with the new 'saw tooth' extended wing leading edge (Mod. 228), and the lengthened cartridge chutes of the '6 just below the air intake. Gun port blast deflectors have still to be fitted in this 1959 photo. (the late Dick Millward)

later changed to black within a white triangle; the letter was usually repeated in white on a black nose wheel door, beneath which there was often a miniature unit marking of a white triangle, within the fine white outline of a rectangle.

3 Squadron
Markings, F.4s:

Light green rectangles, thinly outlined in yellow, each side of the fuselage roundel, above the centre line. Some F.4s had a very small squadron badge on each side of the nose, beneath the cockpit. One aircraft, XF990/K was adopted by the Geilenkirchen Wing Leader, Wg. Cdr. Bob Weighill, DFC, and carried miniature markings of 2,3, and 234 Squadrons, beneath one another on the nose, immediately ahead of a wing commander's pennant.

Code Letters

Red, outlined in white, angular in style and quite large, above and behind the fin flash. Letter repeated in black (?) on the nose wheel door.

4 Squadron
Markings, F.4s:

Rectangles comprising black (upper) and red (lower) segments, divided diagonally by a yellow lightning flash, and outlined in yellow, were applied each side of the fuselage roundel, on the centreline. On each side of the nose, beneath the cockpit, was a black

Close-up of the markings of a 4 Sqn Hunter F.4 in early 1956 (Robin Brown)

sunburst device, derived from the squadron badge, within which a red '4' was pierced by a yellow lightning flash. Some aircraft carried the pilot's name beneath the cockpit in white.

Code Letters

Yellow, and later white, above and behind the fin flash, probably repeated on the nose wheel door, colours unknown.

Markings, F.6s:

Instead of the rectangular markings adjacent to the fuselage roundel, the same design, but much reduced in size, was re-positioned to the nose, on either side of the black sunburst, pierced '4', and lightning flash. White fuselage serial numbers were later introduced, and a very small Union flag was applied to each side of the nose during the latter period of service.

Code Letters

White, above and behind the fin flash, repeated in black on the white nose wheel door.

Markings FR.10s & T.7s:

The nose markings of the F.6s were retained, but in addition the larger squadron rectangles were reinstated on each side of the fuselage roundel, but raised above the centreline. Pilots' names, in white above the unit markings on the nose, were adopted in the later '60s. Some aircraft also featured white serial numbers, rather than black, on the rear fuselage.

Code Letters

White, above and behind fin flash, repeated in white on a red nose wheel door.

14 Squadron

Markings, F.4s:

White rectangles, each containing three medium blue diamonds, applied either side of the fuselage roundel, on the centreline. The squadron emblem, initially within a blue disc, later changed to white, thinly outlined in black, was positioned on each side of the nose.

Code Letters

White, above and behind the fin flash, and repeated in blue on white nose wheel door.

Markings, F.6s:

Initially the markings on each side of the fuselage similar to those used on the F.4s, were retained; however these were later re-positioned above the centreline. The squadron emblem was also deleted from the nose, although later re-introduced in less conspicuous form, without white disc background. White serial numbers rather than black, were adopted on the rear fuselage. Pilots' names were also featured from about 1960 on most aircraft, above the squadron emblem on the nose.

Code Letters

Initially, black letter within a white disc above and behind the fin flash but later these colours were reversed, and repeated in blue on a white nose wheel door, with some aircraft featuring the miniature markings of three blue diamonds beneath the letter.

20 Squadron

Markings, F.4s:

Royal Blue rectangles, divided horizontally by thin stripes of red, white, and green, were applied to each side of the fuselage roundel, on the centreline.

Code Letters

White, in front of the fin flash, repeated in black on the nose wheel door.

Markings, F.6s:

The rectangular fuselage markings, and code letters were retained as per those on the F.4s. The wing tips were, however, painted yellow and pilots' and ground crews' names were painted in white beneath the cockpit windscreen.

(Top) Hunter F.4 XE657 'Y' of 14 Sqn Oldenburg February 1956, complete with markings, badge, link collector tanks and extended cartridge chutes. (P. Fehlauer)(Centre) 14 Sqn F.6 XJ642 'A' seconds from touch down at Gütersloh. Embodying saw-tooth wing leading edge and fitted with inboard 100 gal. Bristol plastic drop tanks without fins, it retains the early squadron markings on the centre line. (Günther Kipp)

(Bottom) Showing the final form of 14 Sqn Hunter F.6 markings, XJ712 'B' carries the name of the C.O. Sqn Ldr E. H. Williams beneath the cockpit together with the squadron's emblem and badge, which unusually is also repeated just ahead of the fuselage serial number. This was one the last F.6s to leave Gütersloh, on 14 February 1963, after disbandment. (via Geoff Cruikshank)

(Above) Hunter F.6 XJ680 'A' 20 Sqn on finals to Gütersloh in June 1959. This aircraft is still without some of the late modifications, including stabilising fins on the 100 gal. drop tanks, gun blast deflectors, Rebecca 8 and Green Salad. In contrast to the Hunter 4s previously operated by the squadron, the wing tips have been painted yellow, although otherwise markings and the style and colour of code letters remain unchanged. (via E. Westersotebier)

(Right) Hunter F.4 WV408 'U' of 20 Sqn on a rainy winter's day at Oldenburg in February 1956. (P.Fehlauer)

(Below) F.6 XJ712 'F' of 20 Sqn on Gütersloh's runway in March 1959, fitted with extended wing leading edges, and also sporting yellow wing tips and pilot's bone dome helmet. This aircraft is illustrated earlier in this book when serving with 14 Sqn three years later (via E.Westersotebier)

(Above) Hunter F.4 XE668 'G' of 26 Sqn taxies back to dispersal at Oldenburg, with German AVTAG refuelling bowser in hot pursuit. (Right) The young pilot, Fg Off R. J.(Bob) Chase, clambers out, having already handed his bone dome to one of the waiting ground crew. The aircraft still lacks link collectors and must therefore have been photographed soon after delivery in June 1955. (Mike Hall)

(Above) During its time with Hunter 4s 26 Sqn used at least two different types of Springbok markings, one of which is shown here with Fg Off John Merry on the ladder of Fg Off Robert Snare's aircraft. (Alan Pollock)

(Right) Fg Off Mike Hall beside his Hunter F.6 of 26 Sqn showing the crisp, 'hard' edged detailing of the Springbok's head which characterised the first form of squadron markings on this mark. (Mike Hall)

(Left) When HRH the Duke of Edinburgh visited Oldenburg in 1956, 26 Sqn had the honour of showing him this immaculate example of their Hunter 4s. 26 was the only Oldenburg unit to carry its markings and badge on the nose of their Hunters. (Archiv P. Fehlauer)

(Below left) Nigel Walpole's F.4 WV255 'X' in which the Springbok's head is more detailed. The pilot is Fg Off Bill Bailey whose outstretched hand and thumb indicate that as leader of a section or a pair he is ready to start: after getting all the thumbs up he would just close his thumb back into his palm and then give two distinctive, circular, vertical, sweeps of his index finger and hand as the order to start up. (Alan Pollock)

26 Squadron
Markings, F.4s:

Black rectangles, outlined in yellow and containing a green lightning flash were applied to the forward nose on either side of a white disc, which was ringed in dark blue, and finely outlined in pale blue. Within the disc a Springbok's head was painted in brown, grey, and black detail, adapted from the squadron badge. The Springbok faced forward on the port side, and aft on the starboard side of the nose; variations occurred in the style and size of Springbok's head.

Code Letters

Yellow, angular in type style, above and behind the fin flash, repeated in black on the silver or white nose wheel door, although some aircraft had a light (white ?) code letter on black (?) nose wheel door, possibly indicating assignment to 'A' or 'B' Flights.

Markings, F.6s:

Much enlarged rectangular markings, thinly outlined in yellow, on each side of the nose, with the green lightning flashes pointing in the opposite direction to those used on the F.4s. The large white disc, thinly outlined in brick red/brown, featured a larger Springbok's head in black, grey, beige, and brown, and faced forward on the port side of the aircraft, and aft on the starboard. Two versions of the Springbok's head marking existed: one (probably the first) featured a very detailed, 'hard' rendition, while the other was in a 'softer' focus, more impressionist style.

Code Letters

Yellow, thinly outlined in green, were retained on the fin, and repeated in the same colours on the nose wheel door, usually with the addition, below the letter, of a miniature rectangular squadron marking.

67 Squadron
Markings, F.4s:

Very small red rectangles, each containing a blue horizontal triangle, outlined in yellow, each side of a simplistic squadron badge, were applied to the nose beneath the cockpit. The pilot's name was painted in very small

(Above left) 26 Sqn F.6 XF419 'J' at Gütersloh, with saw-tooth wings, but no gun blast deflectors or fins on the drop tanks. (Roger Lindsay collection)

(Left) Detail of the 'soft focus' version of Springbok markings that were seen on some of 26 Sqn's F.6s. (Archiv W. Moll)

(Above) Hunter F.4 XF313 'G' of 71 Sqn Brüggen seen during an APC at Sylt during the winter of 1956/57. Note the tail prop positioned beneath the rear fuselage to prevent the aircraft from tail-sitting when the heavy gun pack was temporarily removed from the nose, even though it was usual for only 25 or 50 rounds per gun to be carried during each APC sortie, and only one or two guns fired. (Robin Brown)

(Right) 71 Sqn moved their markings from the fuselage to the nose of their Hunters by early 1957, either side of a white disc containing an American eagle, in black with yellow detailing as seen on 'M'. (Robin Brown)

(Below Right) Hunter 4 XF296 'Z' of 67 Sqn at Brüggen in '56 sports probably the smallest markings of any RAF Hunter squadron. Note the new gun pack extreme right, and pale blue code letter on the nose wheel door, which was also painted on the fin; the squadron markings, rather crudely stencilled below the cockpit, comprise red rectangles, containing a blue horizontal triangle outlined in yellow surmounted with a simplistic badge. (Robin Brown)

white or yellow (?) lettering beneath the canopy sill.

Code Letters

Pale blue, above and behind the fin flash, repeated in pale blue on the nose wheel door.

71 Squadron

Markings, F.4s:

Rectangles centred on each side of the fuselage roundel comprised white (upper) and yellow (lower) halves, on which two black diamonds were superimposed. Prior to disbandment these rectangular markings were reduced in size, and moved to the nose, on either side of a white disc containing an American eagle emblem in black, with red and yellow detailing.

Code Letters

Angular in style, applied in yellow above and behind the fin flash, and repeated in black on the nose wheel door.

(Top) During their time with Hunter 4s the markings of 98 Sqn never changed. (Brian Sharman)

(Above) Details of 93 Sqn's blue and yellow markings on Hunter 4 XE718 'A' used by the C.O. Sqn Ldr D.F.M. Browne. (Robin Brown)

93 Squadron
Markings, F.4s:

Royal Blue rectangles, outlined in yellow, and each containing a stylised arrowhead device in yellow, were applied either side of the fuselage roundels, on the centreline. On the nose, beneath the cockpit, was the escarbuncle design derived from the Squadron badge, in yellow on a blue disc, with a yellow outline.

Code Letters

Yellow, above and behind the fin flash, repeated in black on the nose wheel door.

Markings, F.6s:

Compared with the attractive livery of the F.4s the F.6s initially carried only the diminutive escarbuncle design on the nose; later the blue and yellow rectangular arrowhead markings were added either side of this, but were small and insignificant compared with the décor of the F.4s. Later still a small Union flag was painted on the nose aft of the radome. The pilot's name, in yellow on a blue stripe was positioned above the nose markings, beneath which the inscription '93 SQUADRON' appeared in yellow on a blue stripe. Wing tips were later painted yellow, and fuselage serial numbers were changed from black to white.

Code Letters

Yellow, later thinly outlined in dark

XF 937 'T' a Hunter 4 of 112 Sqn at Brüggen in August 1956. (Robin Brown)

blue, above and behind the fin flash, initially repeated in yellow on the (silver) nose wheel door; later the background colour of the nose door was changed to dark blue.

98 Squadron
Markings, F.4s:
Red rectangles, containing a white zig-zag, were positioned either side of the fuselage roundel, on the centreline. A miniature form of these markings, on each side of a small white disc containing the Squadron badge, was repeated on the nose, beneath the cockpit.
Code Letters
White, above and behind the fin flash, repeated in black on the nose wheel door.

112 Squadron
Markings, F.4s:
Sharksteeth marking in white, black, and red underneath the nose forward of the wings, with similarly coloured 'eye' beneath the cockpit.
Code Letters
White, aft of the fuselage roundel, repeated in red on the nose wheel door.

118 Squadron
Markings, F.4s:
White wavy 'rectangles' comprising two black wavy lines, on each side of the

(Above) Line up of 93 Sqn's Hunter F.6s for the AOC's inspection on 6 May 1960 at Jever, exhibiting the later unit markings, including the inscription '93 Squadron' beneath the nose marking, and the Union Jack on the nose of some aircraft. Wing tips are yellow, as are the fin code letters, thinly outlined in blue. (Mick Ryan)

The following six pictures below all originate from Robin Brown, 'A' Flt Cdr of 112 Sqn and redoubtable photographer (Top left) Robin sits in the cockpit of a 67 Sqn F4, the markings of which are barely visible, in May '57, wearing the early tinted visor that was secured to the bone dome by only a few press-studs. 112 had lost most of its F.4s in April and had to borrow Hunters from other 135 Wing squadrons.

(Centre left) Robin Brown in his 112 Sqn' office'; note the replacement gun packs often

required retrospective repainting of the squadron markings.(Bottom left) Close-up of 130 Sqn markings on an F.4 at Brüggen in 1956. The elephant's head is grey on a white disc flanked by two red triangles on blue rectangles, outlined in white. More detailing was later added to the elephant.

(Top right) 98 Sqn's red and white markings on WT742 'A' in early '56. This Kingston-built F.4 was prematurely scrapped in October '57 despite having low airframe hours.

(Centre right) Close-up of 118 Sqn's black and white markings.

(Bottom right) Close-up of 234 Sqn's red and black diamond markings, with the white outline of the dragon still incomplete.

(Below, left) 234 Sqn's C.O. Sqn Ldr E.A. Riseley putting the finishing touches to the squadron markings on a newly arrived F.4. (Bill Toozs-Hobson)

(Top) Famous markings on 112 Sqn F.4 XF319 '?' at Brüggen in March '56. The idea of substituting a question mark instead of a code letter came as a suggestion from Robin Brown to the C.O., Sqn Ldr C.J. Homes. (Robin Brown)

(Above, centre) Line-up of Hunter 4s of 130 Sqn at Brüggen led by XF295 'C', the code letter of which is encircled in white to signify its allocation to the C.O. (Robin Brown)

(Below, right) Hunter 4 WV332 with '234 F.T.S.' inscription and yellow training bands. This was the idea of 112 Sqn's C.O. when the aircraft was to be transferred to 234 Sqn; however 332 was stopped by Air Traffic Control on the instructions of Brüggen's Station Commander as it taxied out for take-off to Geilers and the 'special markings' were removed before its eventual delivery on 6 May 1957. (Robin Brown)

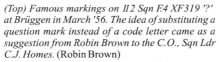

fuselage roundel, on the centreline. These markings were repeated on each side of the nose, in miniature, either side of a white disc containing the Squadron badge.

Code Letters

Yellow, above and behind the fin flash, and repeated in black on the nose wheel door.

130 Squadron
Markings, F.4s:

Applied to the nose, forward of the cockpit, comprising blue rectangles containing a red horizontal triangle, all of which were outlined in white, positioned either side of a white disc, outlined in black, in the centre of which was an elephant's head in grey, black, and brown, adapted from the Squadron's badge; later greater detailing was given to the elephant's head, which faced forward on the port side of the nose, and aft on the starboard. At least some aircraft featured had crew names in white above the nose markings.

Code letters

Quite small, in white, on either a red or a dark blue disc, respectively indicating 'A' Flight (early letters in the alphabet) or 'B' Flight (late alphabet), above and behind the fin flash, and repeated in black on the nose wheel door.

234 Squadron
Markings, F.4s:

Black rectangles, each containing four pairs of red diamonds, were positioned on the nose, either side of a griffon emblem derived from the Squadron badge; the griffon was black, outlined in white, with white, red, and yellow detailing, and faced forward on each side of the aircraft.

Code Letters

White, initially superimposed against a black oblong, later discontinued, and applied above and behind the fin flash; they were repeated in red on the nose wheel door.

Wing Leaders' Aircraft

In addition to the previously mentioned F.4 XF 990 'K' of 3 Squadron,

also used by the Geilenkirchen Wing Leader, at least two other Hunter F.4s, assigned to the Jever Wing Leader, featured special markings. XE665 and XF315 both carried the miniature insignia of Nos. 4, 93, 98, and 118 Squadrons, arranged vertically beneath one another, on each side of the nose, under the cockpit, with a Wing Commander's rank pennant immediately ahead of these. In the case of XE665 the pennant was initially wrongly applied, with the chevron pointing towards the nose of the aircraft, although this was later corrected, while XF315 always depicted the pennant in the approved configuration with the chevron pointing towards the tail. 665's nose wheel door was adorned with small pale yellow and red checks, comprising thirty-three in each colour, the significance of which is so far unconfirmed but is believed to have originated from the primary colours of Nos. 4 and 93 Squadrons. 315 in contrast featured the letters WCW in black, one above another on the nose wheel door, signifying Wing Commander West.

The Wing Leaders at Brüggen and Oldenburg also had their 'own' Hunter 4s; at the former, XE714 was the personal aircraft of Wing Commander ('Peter') Edward Lawley McMillan, AFC, the leader of 135 Wing and wore his initials ELM, on the fin in white as far as he can recall (and just possibly in black on the nose wheel door), while at

Another, slightly different view of 122 Wing Leader Wg Cdr C. S. (Hammer) West in his F4 XE665, which was transferred to 118 Sqn on 17 April 1956, becoming 'A'. (Brian Sharman)

Oldenburg WV260 carried the letters IR-C in white on each side of the fuselage roundel, signifying its allocation to Wg. Cdr. I.R. Campbell. This aircraft, and Wingco was succeeded by XF983 assigned to Wg. Cdr. Plumtree, which carried the Wing Commander's pennant, beneath the cockpit, and below this, in white was the inscription '124 Wing', above the Oldenburg city emblem and below the inscription 'RAF Oldenburg'. 983 also featured white wing tips and a white nose wheel door on which was painted a black triangle.

Laarbruch Hunter T.7s

During the early 1980s when additional Hunters were at Laarbruch, a very small Penguin marking was applied to each side of the nose of some of the based T.7s, apparently the 'trademark' of the Laarbruch Visiting Aircraft Service Section!

Wg Cdr 'Hammer' West's second F4 was XF315 which replaced XE665 in April '56 and remained in use as the Jever Wing Leader's aircraft until August '57. The nose markings of the four squadrons at Jever were slightly revised and the nose wheel door carried the black letters 'WCW' indicating Wg Cdr West. (W.Zucht)

(Above) Wg Cdr 'Hammer' West in his second Hunter 4, XF315, tucked in tightly beside the Meteor T.7 'photo ship', showing the smaller Wing Commander's pennant (with the chevron now facing the correct way) and the revised 4 and 93 Sqn markings which are now thinly outlined in yellow. (W.Zucht)

(Below) Close-up of the original presentation of markings on the nose of Hunter F.4 XE665, assigned to Wg Cdr C. S. West as 122 Wing Leader, prior to the fitment of 'Sabrina' link collectors. The pennant's chevron incorrectly faces forward instead of aft, while the nose wheel door is decorated with 33 sets of red and yellow chequers, colours which similarly adorned 'Hammer' West's bone dome. (Brian Sharman)

(Above) Hunter F.4 XF990 'K' of 3 Sqn also used by Geilenkirchen's 138 Wing Leader Wg Cdr R. (Bob) G. Weighill, and decorated with miniature replicas of 2, 3, and 234 Sqns' markings immediately ahead of his wing commander's pennant, taxying out on 11 April 1957. (Danny Lavender)

(Right) In 1956/57 this Hunter 4 was used by Wg Cdr Plumtree, then Wing Leader at Oldenburg. It sported white wing tips and on the nose the Wing Commander's pennant, above what can only be guessed as the wording '124 Wing', below which was the Oldenburg coat of arms and the wording 'RAF Oldenburg'. A black triangle was painted on the (white ?) nose wheel door. (H. Weichardt)

(Below) In somewhat less flamboyant fashion, the Wing Leader of Oldenburg's 124 Wing, Wg Cdr I. R. Campbell, used his initials, in white, to flank the roundels of his Hunter 4 WV260, used between 18 July 1955 and 19 July 1956. (P. Fehlauer)

Aerobatics

With the command expanding and new squadrons forming on many airfields, by the middle of 1956 the Hawker Hunter was the most numerous type of aircraft, and so it was only a question of time that the general exuberance, coupled with official encouragement and examples set by Fighter Command, would lead to the formation of aerobatics teams and solo aerobatics exponents with this aircraft which was, as it quickly transpired, superbly suited for this purpose.

Almost all Hunter stations sported at least one aerobatics team and pilots specialising in solo aerobatics. With such a wealth of talent available it was decided that 2TAF should have both an official aerobatics team and also a solo aerobatics display pilot, to represent the Command at the numerous air shows right across the Continent.

Competitions were held in 1956 and 1957 and on both occasions it was representatives from 122 Wing at Jever, who came out on top. 93 Sqn's aerobatics team with Hunter F.4s led by the C.O. Sqn Ldr Desmond F.M. Browne, and in 1957 by his successor as C.O., Sqn Ldr H."Paddy" Minnis, shared the honour with Flt Lt Ken Goodwin of 118 Sqn as solo aerobatics pilot, using Hunter 4s in 1956 and Hunter F.6s in 1957. A closer look at the preparations and build-up to the 1957 display season, as recalled by

Paddy Minnis gives a good idea of the efforts required to achieve a standard admired both by fellow pilots and the display audiences.

Sqn Ldr Minnis led his team, which included Flt Lt C. R."Taff" Taylor, No. 2, Fg Off R "Clam" Clayton-Jones, No 3, and Fg Off Sandy Sanderson, No 4, on their first practice sortie on 21 January 1957. On this and subsequent sorties until March, the team was still flying Hunter 4s. Although Nos 3 and 4 had flown in the previous year's team, the No 2 had no previous experience. The leader, who had taken over as Squadron Commander in December 1956 had flown as No 2 in 54 Sqn's Vampire team in the 1950 RAF display at Farnborough.

The first practice and a further seven the following week were authorised to be flown at a minimum altitude of 10,000 ft; also the leader had flown two solo aerobatics sorties to ensure that the manoeuvres were performed as smoothly as possible.

Normal squadron activities ruled out a practice for the whole of February but in March, with the height limitation reduced to 2,000 ft, another eight practice sorties produced a flowing sequence of manoeuvres in a tightened display pattern. April with 27 sorties in their brand new Hunter F.6s and the height restriction further reduced to 500 ft brought the required polishing to prepare the team for the said inter-

(Left) Going vertical. Ken Goodwin demonstrates the Hunter's impressive rate of climb on his way to a loop in WT743 'R' of 118 Sqn (Ken Goodwin via Andy Thomas)

(Right) Virtuoso solo aerobatics performer (then Flt Lt, later Air Cdr) Ken Goodwin, AFC, 'B' Flt Cdr of 118 Sqn about to enter the cockpit of a 93 Sqn Hunter F6 for another superlative exhibition. (Ken Goodwin)

squadron competition to be held at Gütersloh on 1 May. Also in April the leader had flown another six solo trips concentrating on the positioning of the display relative to the spectators.

After beating the other competitors at Gütersloh and five more practices the team took off for their first public display of the season at USAF Spangdahlem on 17 May, at Etain in France the following day and eventually USAF Bitburg on 19 May. Shortly after arriving at Spangdahlem the team flew a practice sortie when, tragically, after a "bomb burst" and while rejoining formation, the No 4, Fg Off Sanderson struck the ground and was killed immediately. Courageously, the following three displays were flown with three aircraft.

In the following weeks, Fg Off G W "Geoff" Timms flew 9 practice sorties as No 2 and, now restored to four, the team flew to Soesterberg in Holland for a display at The Hague on 10 June. The Anglo-German week at Jever required another display on 19 June and on 23

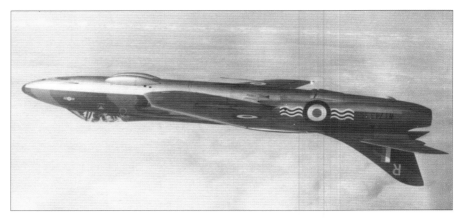

(Top) Hunter F.4 WT743 'R' of 118 Sqn, flown by Flt Ken Goodwin, seen inverted above the clouds during aerobatics practice in the summer of 1956. (Brian Sharman)

June poor weather led to a limited programme at Lyon.

Further displays were given over Cannes harbour on 25 August and during the Anglo-German week at Sylt on 29 August. Then on the 4 September, the team with all the required ground equipment took off for their final display, this time in support of the British Trade Fair at Helsinki in Finland, with refuelling stops at Vaerlose in Denmark and Barkaby in Sweden. Displays over Helsinki harbour on 6 and 7 September were followed by an unscheduled show, especially requested by the Royal Swedish Air Force on 9 September at the home of F 8 Wing, Barkaby, which was then equipped with J 34 Hunters. On 10 September the formation aerobatics season ended when the team landed at Jever after having flown some 90 practice and display sorties throughout six European countries.

There were two notable features in the 93 Sqn aerobatics team performance: firstly, only a few seconds after "wheels up" one notch of flap was selected and was used right through to the approach for landing. This gave the pilots more immediate engine reaction, operating at higher revs, and enabled them to fly the display in a smaller air space. Secondly, immediately after take-off in "box" formation at some 270 knots, usually a few hundred yards beyond the end of the runway, the team could pull up into a loop and roll-off the top to return over the runway at low level. Obviously this manoeuvre was only possible with the more powerful Hunter F.6.

An unusual incident occurred during the April practice sorties when after landing the No 4 aircraft's rudder

(Below) Members of the 93 Sqn aerobatic team, June 1957, l. to r. Fg Off R. (Clam) Clayton-Jones (No.4), Sqn Ldr H. (Paddy) Minnis (C.O. and Leader), Fg Off G. (Geoff) W. Timms (No.2), and Flt Lt C. R. (Taff) Taylor (No.3); note the blue bone domes with yellow arrows. (W.Zucht)

(Below, right) 93 Sqn aerobatic team in action over the Helsinki waterfront in September 1957 in their Hunter 6s led by Sqn Ldr 'Paddy' Minnis. (via Alan Pollock)

jammed and the subsequent investigation revealed that the mass balance weight fixed to the top of the rudder and located within the fin, had fallen off the rudder. The balance weight had been crystallised as a result of the No 4 being so close to the leader in the line astern position that the top of No 4's fin was being "cooked" by the leader's jet efflux. As the No 4 generally flew this particular aircraft whenever possible, and as no other aircraft had this rudder problem, the simple remedy was for the No 4 to position himself a few feet lower in the line astern position. This adjustment had the additional effect of removing the occasional upward pressure on the tail of the leader's aircraft, which he had found disconcerting at times.

Finally it is worth stating that the team was allowed almost as much time as they felt was needed for practising, obviously consistent with remaining proficient in the other aspects of their job. They never assumed an official name for the team, preferring to use the squadron identity.

The fact that the solo aerobatics displays were also provided by a pilot of 122 Wing Jever, namely Flt Lt Goodwin of 118 Sqn, came in quite handy, as it enabled both "teams" to travel together and possibly simplify the logistics. Their co-operation even went so far, that Ken Goodwin used a Hunter F.6 of 93 Sqn for his solo displays during the 1957 season (118 Sqn never re-equipped with Hunter 6s), which enabled him to show off the superior performance of the new aircraft.

His display started in a most spectacular manoeuvre when shortly after lift-off he inverted his Hunter and only retracted the undercarriage when the aircraft was in the inverted position. The inverted climb and pull through went over into a slow roll and was followed by a horizontal figure 8 using Derry turns. A wing-over preceded an eight point hesitation roll, and the display ended with a vertical figure 8 which included a loop, and as spectacular as the take-off, was the last manoeuvre of an inverted break for landing.

Often the display, which lasted seven and a half to eight minutes, started with a sonic boom from 40,000 ft. after which the Hunter, diving supersonically, had to stay ahead of the boom. After levelling out over the display area and flying below the speed of sound now, it was still ahead of the sonic boom and the uninformed spectators were tricked into believing that the Hunter was supersonic straight and level. "Beating the boom" was a major attraction and the highlight of many air shows. Maximum Gs pulled was +7 and -3.5 and the fuel consumption was 1,600 lbs.

The 1957 display season more or less coincided with the issue of the Defence White Paper but sensibly official aerobatics, so admirably presented by 122 Wing Jever, were allowed to continue to the end of the season in September, but the much reduced size of 2TAF did not seem to justify the "extravagance" of official aerobatics and its brilliant performances were never to be watched again. Perhaps it serves as a consolation, that Hunters were the last to perform so outstandingly in this role.

Armament Practice Station RAF Sylt

The only air-to-air firing range in 2TAF was over the North Sea off the North Frisian island of Sylt, and as such it was regularly used by Hunter 4s and 6s and later FR.10s, as well as by Venoms, Meteors, Sabres, Swifts and Javelins. From 1958/59 the Luftwaffe was a

(Top) Meteor F.8 WL131 'N', Target Towing Squadron, APS Sylt showing the standard scheme in 1957/8 of overall High Speed Silver with yellow training bands around outer wings and rear fuselage, and yellow under surfaces with diagonal black target towing stripes. The aircraft serial number was stencilled in black on the yellow nose wheel door. (Peter Sawyer)

(Above) Meteor F.8 WL189 'A', TTS, taxies out at Sylt. It has a narrow rear fuselage yellow band, and RAF Sylt badge which most of the Squadron's F.8s displayed on each side of the nose. (Peter Sawyer)

(Right) Flt Lt Peter Sawyer climbs aboard F.8 WF715 'M' of the TTS, with WK930 'Y' in the background. (Peter Sawyer)

(Below) Meteor F.8 WK815 'R', unusually in the Dark Green / Dark Sea Grey fighter camouflage but with target towing stripes, taxies from the busy TTS flight line, which includes a T.7 and gun-blackened F.8 WH300 'C'. (Peter Sawyer)

regular user with F-84Fs and Sabre 5s and 6s and the Belgian Air Force used it with Meteors, Hunters, F and RF-84Fs, and CF-100s - they even had their own towing flight of four Meteor 8s.

Each 2TAF Hunter squadron usually had two PAIs (Pilot Attack Instructors) among its complement of pilots, and these were heavily involved in both the preparatory training and the actual APC detachments to Sylt, generally of 4 weeks' duration, twice a year. Upon arrival at Sylt one, and sometimes two initial sorties were flown in dual-controlled Vampire T.11 s to give live firing experience with a PAI from the resident Weapons Training Squadron - occasionally referred to as 402 WTS - a designation that is believed to have originated simply because the hangar from which it operated was building No.402 ! (From the autumn of 1957 until June '59 two Hunter F.4s were also used by the WTS, and from early in 1959 Hunter T.7s supplemented the Vampires, some of which remained in use until September 1961). The all-important task of target towing was the responsibility of Sylt's Target Towing Squadron (TTS), and such was the demand for its services that it had a unit establishment of 26 Meteor F.8s, plus two Meteor T.7s for dual checks, instrument ratings and continuation training. It was also a Reserve fighter squadron, and its pilots had to remain operational, while range safety was a prime responsibility with TTS Meteors tasked to fly a shipping search every hour during firing operations. Almost invariably these were flown at low level, often with one engine shut down to extend endurance! If a ship was sighted in the vicinity of any of the ranges its position and heading would be radioed to the covering GCI station, the onus being on the APS to ensure no firing took place if any shipping was in the area. A TTS Meteor would also fly a weather reconnaissance sortie every morning before any firing took place.

Pilots from the visiting squadrons then practised cine quarter attacks in their own Hunters, often as early as their second or third day at Sylt, initially at altitudes below 10,000 ft. and then up to 20,000 ft or above, subject to the weather, at any of Sylt's five air-to-air ranges. Operating as a pair, the Hunters would take up a 'perch' above and behind the Meteor 8 tug aircraft, and

when cleared would call 'in, cine' or 'in, live' and half roll in a dive towards the towed target, invariably heading out to sea. Another golden rule was never to fly beneath the target during a firing pass. Usually three or four such attacks could be made during one sortie, mostly against flag targets, but sometimes target gliders were available, mainly reserved for the more experienced or higher scoring pilots, one of whom described the experience as 'marvelous fun, because you could see the bullets strike home, often inflicting structural damage that caused the glider to spin in'.

Early Vampire T.11 WZ454 'A' of the Weapons Training Squadron, APS Sylt. This was one of the first three T.11s delivered to the unit on 26 November 1952, with heavily framed canopy and no ejection seats, and it remained on Sylt strength until August 1956 when it went to Marshalls, Cambridge to receive a major modification upgrade to rectify these deficiencies. (Brian Sharman)

A Meteor F.8 of the TTS towing a flag target past a lighthouse at Sylt. Target gliders were also used, (but to a much lesser extent), in addition to the cheaper and more durable flag or banner targets, which were attached to a lug fitted to the Meteor's ventral tank at the end of a cable that was laid out on the runway, and 'flown off' as the Meteor became airborne. (Archive W. Moll)

Peter Sawyer, a TTS Meteor pilot from September 1957 until June 1958 recalls: *"Occasionally, if the fighters made too shallow an angle of attack you could actually see bullets going past your aeroplane, but nobody took too much notice of such things in those days!"* After the conclusion of a towing sortie the Meteor would return to Sylt and release the target flag from 500 ft. above the airfield where it would be retrieved and the scores examined. An APC at Sylt required much prior planning as the visiting squadrons were self-contained, and brought with them their own vitally important ground crews to service and arm the aircraft, together with the associated equipment, all of which had to be transported by road or rail across the Hindenburg dam between Niebüll and Westerland.

Being one of the most popular holiday resorts on the North Sea and favouring co-operation from the local population, whose patience was occasionally tested beyond what could reasonably be expected, good public relations were of the essence, and so Open Days were held, quite unusually for the fifties, in 1957 and 1959. These were nothing if not spectacular, as the visiting squadrons took part in the demonstrations. In 1957 it was the massed take-off of four squadrons which started the flying activities: 256 Sqn from Ahlhorn with Meteor NF.11s, 29 Sqn BAF with Meteor 8s, Sylt TTS with Meteor F.8s and 4 Sqn from Jever with Hunter F.6s. The spectacle of some 50 aircraft taking off simultaneously is a rare sight which crowds are unlikely ever to watch again. The "normal" flying programme included demonstrations by Sycamores, Vampire T.11s, Mosquito, Canberra, Venom, Swift and F-84F and last but not least 93 Sqn's Hunter F.6 aerobatic team and 118 Sqn's Flt Lt Goodwin with his unique solo display.

1959's Open Day was equally impressive as it sported participants from the UK such as 111Sqn's "Black Arrows" and the fly-past of a white Vulcan bomber. Hunter T.7's were involved for the first time and the massed take-off included 26 Sqn from Gütersloh with Hunter F.6s, Sylt TTS with Meteor F.8s and Sabre 5s from the Luftwaffe OCU at Oldenburg. RAF Sylt was transferred to the Luftwaffe by the end of 1961, which continued to use it for air-to-air firing, but on a much reduced scale, using just two Sabre 6s as target towing aircraft.

Station Flights
The principal tasks of the Station Flights were to provide aircraft for instrument ratings, continuation training, and communications to meet the needs of the base and its constituent squadrons, which until 1954/55 had usually had their own aircraft for the first two duties. By 1955/56 the dual-controlled Vampire T.11 was the main type used by the Station Flights on Hunter bases in Germany, having displaced the Meteor T.7 which had previously fulfilled this

(Top) The C.O. of the Oldenburg Station Flight, Flt Lt Derek Morter with his ground crew in front of one of their four Vampire T.11s. The Flight's emblem on the nose was derived from the crest of the Oldenburg region, but variations occurred on other T.11s of the unit, as shown below. (Derek Morter)

(Above) Another Oldenburg Station Flight Vampire T.11, WZ501 displaying a different version of the town's emblem on its nose. (the late Arthur Pearcy)

role during the Sabre/Venom era. Most Station Flights also had an Avro Anson for communications, and quite often a Chipmunk primary training aircraft to enable pilots who were on a ground tour to maintain their flying currency; the Station Flight was also usually responsible for maintaining the Hunter assigned to the Wing Leader. From 1959 the Hunter T.7 supplemented and then replaced the Vampire T.11, although by then only two operational Hunter F.6

bases remained in Germany.

Vampire T'11's operated by these Station Flights were finished in overall High Speed Silver with Golden Yellow training bands around wings and rear fuselage booms; each Station Flight usually identified its aircraft with the unit title and/or marking on the nose, and in this respect Oldenburg had several variations, while the T.11's at Brüggen were inscribed INSTRUMENT RATING FLIGHT RAF BRÜGGEN on each side of the nose.

(Below) Vampire T.11 XH309 of RAF Brüggen Instrument Rating Flight, 1956. (MAP)

Individual Histories of Hunters Based in Germany

HUNTER F.4s

3 Sqn.

	Arr.	Dep	
XE715 L	22.6.56	12.12.56	130 Sqn
XF359 L	12.12.56	6.6.57	5 MU
XF360	1.5.57	6.6.57	229 OCU
XF363	14.12.56	6.6.57	5 MU
XF364	7.5.57	21.5.57	5 MU
XF368 C	15.3.57	6.6.57	5 MU
XF946 E	1.5.57	12.6.57	5 MU
XF947 S	6.6.56	6.6.57	5 MU
XF948 J	6.6.56	12.6.57	5 MU
XF949 C	27.6.56	11.1.57	Cat.5
XF950 M	14.8.56	2.5.57	5 MU
XF951 P	6.6.56	6.6.57	229 OCU
XF967 Z	14.6.56	21.6.57	5 MU
XF968 R	6.6.56	7.5.57	5 MU
XF969 D	6.6.56	10.10.56	Cat.4 to HAL
XF971 K	6.6.56	17.12.56	Cat.3 to HAL
XF972 V	22.6.56	6.6.57	26 Sqn.
XF974 G	27.6.56	16.5.57	26 Sqn.
XF975 W	22.6.56	21.6.57	229 OCU
XF976 B	14.6.56	6.6.57	229 OCU
XF990 K	27.7.56	14.8.56	W/L Geil.
XF990K	25.2.57	6.6.57	229 OCU

4 Sqn.

	Arr.	Dep	
WT777 U	20.7.55	15.3.57	98 Sqn.
WT799	22.7.55	6.3.56	Cat.4 to HAL
WT801	27.7.55	20.3.57	229 OCU
WV253 G	25.7.55	25.4.56	Cat.3 to UK
WV263	12.7.55	15.3.57	118 Sqn.
WV266 T	11.7.55	14.3.57	67 Sqn.
WV271	12.7.55	22.10.55	Cat.5
WV274	25.7.55	15.3.57	118 Sqn.
WV275 D	27.7.55	22.3.57	229 OCU
WV279	22.7.55	15.3.57	229 OCU
WV316 D	22.7.55	15.3.57	98 Sqn.
WV321 B	?	?	?
WV368	4.10.55	20.10.55	118 Sqn.
WW647	26.9.55	3.10.55	98 Sqn.
WW654	26.9.55	4.10.55	98 Sqn.
XE663 V	20.7.55	21.3.57	UK 43 Sqn.
XE666 X	11.7.55	21.3.57	UK 245 Sqn.
XE667 Z	12.7.55	15.3.57	98 Sqn.
XE668 X	?	?	?
XE677 M	2.9.55	17.10.55	118 Sqn.
XE684	3.10.55	20.12.55	118 Sqn.
XE703 J	2.9.55	3.2.56	93 Sqn.
XF368 C	27.4.56	15.3.57	3 Sqn.
XF370 Z	27.4.56	14.3.57	118 Sqn.
XF984	9.7.56	25.3.57	71 Sqn.

14 Sqn.

	Arr.	Dep	
WT711 A	8.6.55	24.6.57	5 MU
WT712 D	3.6.55	31.5.57	5 MU
WT714 F	13.6.55	18.8.55	Cat.5
WT723 T	13.5.55	18.4.57	UK
WT745 E	13.5.55	12.4.57	UK 5 MU
WT749 P	13.5.55	15.4.57	UK 5 MU
WT755 Q	23.5.55	18.4.57	UK 5 MU
WT761 O	16.5.55	1.5.57	UK 5 MU
WT767 C	20.5.55	9.4.57	UK
WT797 Z	17.6.55	9.4.57	UK
WT806	20.5.55	17.6.55	Cat.3 to HAL
WT807	3.6.55	18.8.55	Cat.5
WV259	19.7.55	26.4.57	UK
WV267	24.9.55	18.1.56	93 Sqn.
WV277 K	19.9.55	17.1.56	93 Sqn.
WV318	?	?	93 Sqn.
WV377 W	10.9.55	7.11.55	26 Sqn.
WW663 H	24.5.55	18.4.57	5 MU
XE657 Y	13.6.55	12.4.57	UK
XE708	18.10.55	15.4.57	229OCU
XE710 R	18.10.55	25.4.57	5MU

(Above) Hunter F.4 WW656 'N' of 98 Sqn in a near vertical dive. This aircaft carries the Derby coat of arms just ahead of the squadron markings on the nose. (Brian Sharman)

(Right) Hunter 4 WT797 'Z', 14 Sqn Oldenburg in late 1955; the squadron badge had yet to be applied to the nose. (P.Fehlauer)

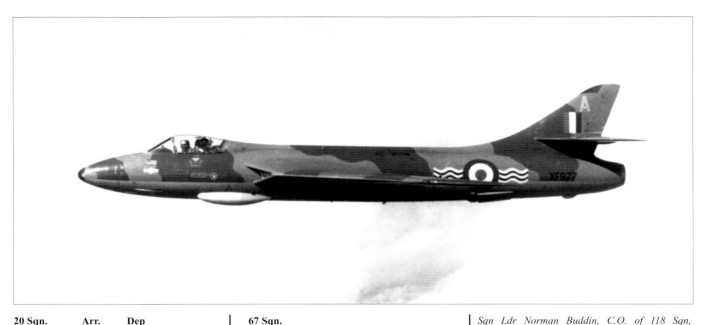

20 Sqn.	Arr.	Dep	
WV261 Y			
WV390G	6.3.56	13.5.57	26 Sqn.
WV391 Z	12.1.56	9.5.57	26 Sqn.
WV394 E	16.12.55	29.4.57	26 Sqn.
WV395 W	9.12.55	13.3.57	Cat.4
WV396 F	4.1.56	9.5.57	26 Sqn.
WV397 B	28.11.55	9.5.57	26 Sqn.
WV398 A	24.11.55	9.5.57	26Sqn.
WV401 T	28.11.55	1.7.57	26 Sqn.
WV407 D or O	9.12.55	11.4.56	Cat. 4
WV408 U	24.11.55	9.5.57	26 Sqn.
WV410 X	29.12.55	9.5.57	26 Sqn.
WV411 D	29.12.55	31.5.57	229OCU
WW589	4.1.56	15.5.57	26 Sqn.
WW590 C	9.12.55	1.7.57	229 OCU
XF978 A	4.7.56	9.5.56	26 Sqn.

26 Sqn.			
WT722 S	29.6.55	17.5.57	5 MU
WT763 A	14.6.55	8.5.57	5 MU
also recorded as coded F.			
WT769 B	17.6.55	1.5.57	5 MU
WT778 W	30.6.55	17.5.57	5 MU
WV255 X	11.7.55	17.5.57	5 MU
WV256 D	13.6.55	26.4.57	5 MU
WV257 E	27.6.55	22.7.55	Cat.4 HAL
WV259	23.6.55	19.7.55	5 MU
WV260 C	19.7.55	8.5.57	5 MU
WV261 Y	12.7.55	15.5.57	5 MU
WV265 V	7.7.55	8.5.57	5 MU
WV268 T	29.6.55	18.6.57	5 MU
WV270 Z	18.7.55	13.5.57	5 MU
WV364	16.9.55	14.11.55	98 Sqn.
WV369 E	27.9.55	17.5.57	5 MU
WV377	7.11.55	16.3.56	93 Sqn.
WV390	13.5.57	20.9.57	RAFFC
WV391	9.5.57	31.5.57	229 OCU
WV394	29.4.57	12.8.57	229 OCU
WV396	9.5.57	12.8.57	5 MU
WV397	9.5.57	31.5.57	5 MU
WV398	9.5.57	20.9.57	229 OCU
WV401	1.7.57	23.10.57	229 OCU
WV408	9.5.57	12.8.57	229 OCU
WV410 B	9.5.57	10.9.57	229 OCU
WW589	15.5.57	12.9.57	229 OCU
WW590	1.7.57	29.9.57	229 OCU
WW664 C	8.6.55	25.5.56	Cat.4
XE664 F	25.6.55	22.8.56	Cat.3 HAL
XE668 G	23.6.55	1.5.57	5 MU
XE670	12.9.55	9.2.56	93 Sqn.
XE675 H	19.9.55	25.11.55	98 Sqn.
XF312	17.5.57	10.9.57	5 MU
XF970	14.5.57	10.9.57	5 MU
XF972	6.6.57	12.9.57	5 MU
XF974	16.5.57	10.5.57	229 OCU
XF978	9.5.57	23.8.57	Cat.3
XF983	4.7.56	9.7.56	W/L Old.
XF983	15.5.57	12.9.57	229 OCU
XF985	14.5.57	10.9.57	5 MU
XF989 A	10.9.56	10.9.57	229 OCU

67 Sqn.			
WV266 B	14.3.57	17.4.57	130 Sqn.
WV273 D	31.3.56	18.4.57	112 Sqn.
WV332 C	12.3.56	18.4.57	112 Sqn.
also recorded as coded X			
WV367 X	25.1.56	17.4.57	130 Sqn.
WV374 L	16.10.56	18.4.57	112 Sqn.
WV382 V	8.3.56	18.4.57	112 Sqn.
also recorded as C			
WV387	10.1.57	8.2.57	71 Sqn.
WV403 J	19.1.56	16.4.57	5 MU
XE689 W	2.3.56	17.4.57	130 Sqn.
coded ELM, re-allocated to 67 Sqn. on			
	4.3.57	18.4.57	112 Sqn.
XE716 A	19.1.56	18.4.57	112 Sqn.
XE717 G	6.3.56	18.4.57	112 Sqn.
XF289 Q	25.1.56	14.12.56	Cat.3 HAL
XF290 F	24.2.56	14.8.56	Cat.5
XF291 E	6.3.56	18.4.57	112 Sqn.
XF296 Z	12.4.56	17.4.57	130 Sqn.
XF305	21.3.56	28.11.56	Cat.5
XF317 U	8.3.56	16.4.57	5 MU

71 Sqn.			
WV384	25.4.56	5.4.57	Cat.5
WV387	8.2.57	20.5.57	5 MU
XF300	14.5.56	30.5.57	234 Sqn.
XF312	14.5.56	8.1.57	112 Sqn.
XF313 G	8.5.56	29.4.57	112 Sqn.
XF316	22.6.56	2.1.57	112 Sqn.
XF362	29.1.57	4.2.57	Cat.4
XF365 B	25.4.56	16.4.57	5 MU
XF366	28.12.56	16.4.57	5 MU
XF367 B	26.4.56	20.11.56	Cat.3 HAL
XF369	26.4.56	4.5.56	234 Sqn.
XF933	25.4.56	17.1.57	Cat.4
XF937	8.1.57	16.4.57	130 Sqn.
XF938 D	25.4.56	15.4.57	5 MU
XF939	10.5.56	12.4.57	5 MU
XF940	24.5.56	15.4.57	5 MU
XF941	27.7.56	15.4.57	5 MU
XF942	25.4.56	15.4.57	5 MU
XF973	10.1.57	15.4.57	5 MU
XF981	6.7.56	17.4.57	5 MU
XF984	25.3.57	16.4.57	5 MU
XF985	20.7.56	10.4.57	5 MU

93 Sqn.			
WV267 R	18.1.56	22.3.57	98 Sqn.
WV277 F	17.1.56	1.4.57	?
WV318 G	?	?	?
WV364 S	28.2.56	12.4.57	98 Sqn.
WV368	18.1.56	22.5.56	118 Sqn.
WV377 V	16.3.56	8.4.57	222 Sqn.
XE670 D	9.2.56	29.3.57	5 MU
XE675 E	18.1.56	1.4.57	229 OCU
XE677 Q	17.1.56	29.3.57	229 OCU
XE684	18.1.56	22.3.57	229 OCU
XE685 B	17.1.56	3.5.56	Cat.4
XE687 C	22.5.56	22.3.57	98 Sqn.

Sqn Ldr Norman Buddin, C.O. of 118 Sqn, anonymous behind his oxygen mask and bone dome, flying straight and level for the benefit of pilot/photographer Brian Sharman of 98 Sqn, both based at 122 Wing, Jever

XE703 P	3.2.56	9.4.57	118 Sqn.
XE707 T	19.4.56	22.3.57	98 Sqn.
XE718 A	12.3.56	27.3.57	98 Sqn.
XF987 O	23.7.56	1.4.57	118 Sqn.

98 Sqn.			
WT742 A	25.4.55	9.4.57	Cat.4 HAL
WT747 B	25.4.55	12.4.57	5 MU
WT777 F	15.3.57	15.7.57	5 MU
WT802 P	12.5.55	9.7.57	5 MU
WV267	22.3.57	9.7.57	5 MU
WV316	15.3.57	17.7.57	5 MU
WV364	14.11.55	18.1.56	118 Sqn.
WV368	7.9.55	4.10.55	4 Sqn.
WV373	7.9.55	4.10.55	118 Sqn.
WV389	14.12.56	26.7.57	229 OCU
WW647 C	21.4.55	10.7.57	5 MU
WW648 D	19.4.55	22.3.57	229 OCU
WW649 E	15.4.55	10.7.57	5 MU
WW650 F	19.4.55	22.3.57	222 Sqn.
WW652 G	19.4.55	29.3.57	222 Sqn.
WW653	21.4.55	8.4.57	5 MU
WW654 L	21.4.55	7.3.56	Cat.4
WW655M	21.4.55	15.7.57	5 MU
WW656 N	20.4.55	8.4.57	5 MU
WW658 O	20.4.55	8.4.57	229 OCU
WW661	21.4.55	3.10.56	Cat.4
XE667 Z	15.3.57	9.7.57	5 MU
XE669	23.7.56	4.12.56	Cat.5
XE675	25.11.55	18.1.56	93 Sqn.
XE684	29.8.55	3.10.55	4 Sqn.
XE685 A	24.8.55	17.1.56	93 Sqn.
XE687 G	22.3.57	25.7.57	5 MU
XE707	22.3.57	18.7.57	5 MU
XE718 A	27.3.57	9.7.57	5 MU
XF996	3.1.57	20.7.57	229 OCU

112 Sqn.			
WV273 D	18.4.57	21.5.57	5 MU
WV332	18.4.57	6.5.57	234 Sqn.
WV374	18.4.57	16.5.57	5 MU
WV382	18.4.57	20.5.57	5 MU
WV412 A	12.4.56	13.9.56	Cat.5
XE672 B	10.4.56	13.5.57	5 MU
XE673 C	12.4.56	2.5.57	234 Sqn.
XE704 S	10.4.56	21.5.57	5 MU
XE714	18.4.57	2.5.57	234 Sqn.
XE715 L	6.5.57	21.5.57	5 MU
XE716 A	18.4.57	14.5.57	5 MU
XE717	18.4.57	25.5.57	234 Sqn.
XF291 E	18.4.57	21.5.57	5 MU
XF292 A	21.5.57	?	5 MU
XF293 N	10.4.56	2.5.57	234 Sqn.
XF294 B	6.5.57	27.5.57	5 MU
XF295 E	6.5.57	19.6.57	5 MU

	Arr.	Dep	
XF296	6.4.56	12.4.57	67 Sqn.
XF306 E	16.4.56	23.4.57	5 MU
XF307 F	20.4.56	21.5.57	5 MU
XF309 C	12.4.56	17.4.57	5 MU
XF311 V	6.5.57	21.6.57	5 MU
XF312 T	8.1.57	17.5.57	26 Sqn.
XF313	29.4.57	?.5.57	5 MU
XF316 R	2.1.57	17.4.57	5 MU
XF319 A	4.12.56	17.4.57	5 MU
XF322 O	20.4.56	17.4.57	5 MU
XF358 P	10.4.56	17.4.57	5 MU
XF362 Q	24.4.56	29.1.57	71 Sqn.
XF366 R	10.4.56	28.12.56	71 Sqn.
XF937 T	24.4.56	8.1.57	71 Sqn.
XF986 A	17.10.56	7.1.57	234 Sqn.

118 Sqn.

	Arr.	Dep	
WT719 L	20.5.55	23.8.55	Cat.4
WT737 N	28.4.55	8.4.57	222 Sqn.
WT738 P	6.5.55	20.10.55	Cat.5
WT741 Q	30.4.55	19.8.57	5 MU
WT743 R	27.4.55	15.3.57	Cat.4
WT748 S	27.4.55	19.8.57	5 MU
WT751 T	27.4.55	24.8.57	5 MU
WT752 D	12.5.55	19.8.57	5 MU
WT753 E	12.5.55	19.8.57	5 MU
WT754 Y	28.4.55	19.8.57	UK
WT757 C	20.4.55	20.10.55	Cat.5
WT760 C	10.5.55	2.4.57	229 OCU
WV263	15.3.57	19.8.57	5 MU
WV274	15.3.57	16.7.57	Cat.4
WV364	18.1.56	28.2.56	93 Sqn.
WV368 F	20.10.55	18.1.56	93 Sqn.
	22.5.56	21.8.57	5 MU
WV373	4.10.55	8.12.55	Cat.5
WW653	3.10.55	4.10.55	98 Sqn.
WW657 G	28.4.55	14.1.57	Cat.4
originally coded A			
WW660 B	27.4.55	29.3.57	229 OCU
XE665 A	17.4.56	13.6.56	Cat.4
XE677	17.10.55	17.1.56	93 Sqn.
XE682 Z	7.3.56	22.10.57	5 MU
XE684	20.12.55	18.1.56	93 Sqn.
XE687 F	28.11.55	22.5.56	93 Sqn.
XE703 B	9.4.57	19.8.57	5 MU
XE707	16.11.55	20.1.56	Cat.3
later to 93 Sqn.			
XF315 A	7.3.56	17.4.56	W/L Jever

Probably the first Hunter to be painted in 130 Sqn. markings, with pilots, including R. N. exchange officer (via Ray Chapman)

	Arr.	Dep	
XF370 C	14.3.57	26.8.57	APS Sylt
XF977 A	23.7.56	14.10.57	APS Sylt
XF987	1.4.57	19.8.57	229 OCU

130 Sqn.

	Arr.	Dep	
WT805 X	10.1.57	2.5.57	234 Sqn.
WV266	17.4.57	2.5.57	234 Sqn.
WV367	17.4.57	2.5.57	234 Sqn.
XE680 Y	21.3.56	2.5.57	234 Sqn.
XE689	17.4.57	2.5.57	234 Sqn.
XE715 L	12.12.56	6.5.57	112 Sqn.
XF292 A	9.4.56	21.5.57	112 Sqn.
XF294 B	6.4.56.	6.5.57	112 Sqn.
XF295 C	9.4.56	6.5.57	112 Sqn.
XF296	17.4.57	2.5.57	234 Sqn.
XF297 D	12.4.56	2.5.57	234 Sqn.
XF298 E	10.4.56	21.5.57	5 MU
XF300 W	27.12.56	6.5.57	5 MU
XF308 F	9.4.56	16.4.57	5 MU
XF311 V	2.1.57	6.5.57	112 Sqn.
XF318 Z	19.4.56	16.4.57	5 MU
XF321 G	10.4.56	16.4.57	5 MU
XF357 T	10.4.56	16.4.57	5 MU
XF359 L	19.4.56	12.12.56	5 MU
XF360	9.4.56	2.1.57	234 Sqn.
XF361	6.4.56	7.8.56	Cat.4 HAL
XF364 X	10.4.56	11.1.57	234 Sqn.
XF937	16.4.57	2.5.57	234 Sqn.
XF970	16.10.56	27.12.56	234 Sqn.

Beautiful inverted four-ship formation of 93 Sqn aerobatic team Hunter F.4s, led by XE718 'A', the C.O.'s aircraft,with WV364 'S', XE703 'P', and XE687 'C' in 1956.(Brian Sharman)

234 Sqn.

	Arr.	Dep	
WT805 J	15.5.56	10.1.57	130 Sqn.
F	2.5.57	9.7.57	5 MU
WV266 B	2.5.57	4.7.57	5 MU
WV332 P	6.5.57	4.7.57	5 MU
WV363 K	15.5.56	2.10.56	Cat.4 HAL
WV367 J	2.5.57	16.8.57	5 MU
WV409 K	14.12.56	26.4.57	229OCU
XE673 E	2.5.57	4.7.57	5 MU
XE674 D	13.4.57	10.5.57	5 MU
XE680 L	2.5.57	4.7.57	5 MU
XE689 K	2.5.57	4.7.57	5 MU
XE714 C	2.5.57	4.7.57	5 MU
XE717 G	25.5.57	4.7.57	5 MU
XF293 N	2.5.57	4.7.57	5 MU
XF296 H	2.5.57	4.7.57	5 MU
XF297 D	2.5.57	4.7.57	5 MU
XF300 P	30.5.57	27.12.56	130 Sqn.
XF311 B	8.5.56	2.1.57	130 Sqn.
XF360 B	2.1.57	1.5.57	3 Sqn.
XF364 J	11.1.57	7.5.57	3 Sqn.
XF369 M	4.5.56	9.7.57	5 MU
XF932 A	10.5.56	21.9.56	Cat.5
XF934 C	10.5.56	6.5.57	5 MU
XF935 D	10.5.56	14.5.57	5 MU
XF936 E	8.5.56	3.6.57	5 MU
XF937 A	2.5.57	9.7.57	5 MU
XF943 F	8.5.56	6.5.57	5 MU
XF944 G	10.5.56	7.5.57	5 MU

2TAF fighters in transition, spring 1956: Sabre F4 XB629 'X' of 3 Sqn, Geilenkirchen soon to be replaced by Hunters, leads a newly delivered Swift FR.5 from the same 138 Wing, while closest to the camera is an equally new Hunter F4, XF309 resplendant in the Sharksteeth markings of 112 Sqn based at Brüggen, soon to be coded 'C'. (via Andy Thomas)

	Arr.	**Dep**	
XF945 H	17.5.56	18.11.56	Cat.5
XF946 L	24.5.56	1.5.57	3 Sq.
XF950	25.5.56	12.6.56	W/L Geil.
XF952 N	29.5.56	18.6.57	5 MU
XF970 P	27.12.56	14.5.57	26 Sqn.
XF986 H	7.1.57	20.5.57	5 MU
XF991 A	23.10.56	7.5.57	5 MU

Wing Leaders

Brüggen
XE714	7.2.56	4.3.57	67 Sqn.

Coded ELM (Wg.Cdr. E.L.McMillan)

Geilenkirchen
XF950	12.6.56	14.8.56	3 Sqn.
XF990	14.8.56	25.2.57	3 Sqn.

coded K of 3 Sqn.

Jever
XE665	20.7.55	17.4.56	118 Sqn.
XF315	17.4.56	23.8.57	5 MU

Oldenburg
WV260	18.7.55	19.7.56	26 Sqn.

coded IRC (Wg. Cdr. I.R.Campbell)
XF983	9.7.56	15.5.57	26 Sqn.

APS RAF Sylt
XF370	26.8.57	22.6.59	19 MU
XF977	14.10.57	22.6.59	19 MU

HUNTER F.6s

2 Sqn.
XG294	1.1.61	10.2.61	5 MU
XJ637	4.1.61	22.2.61	19 MU
XJ639 C	4.1.61	21.3.61	19 MU
XJ645 E	1.1.61	10.2.61	5 MU
XJ676	4.1.61	?	229 OCU

4 Sqn.
	Arr.	**Dep**	
XE548 H	12.2.58	12.1.61	5 MU
XE590 V	10.7.58	9.11.60	Cat.5
XG262 Z	19.3.57	13.6.58	Cat.4 HSA
XG263 G	11.3.57	20.2.61	19 MU
XG267 F	28.2.57	12.1.61	5 MU
XG268 E	28.2.57	12.1.61	5 MU
XG269 W	28.2.57	12.2.61	5 MU
XG270 D	28.2.57	31.5.57	Cat.5
XG293 V	28.2.57	11.6.58	26 Sqn.
XG297 Y	15.3.57	3.1.61	HSA
XG298 X	13.3.57	2.1.61	HSA
XJ636 K	11.3.57	24.7.58	26 Sqn.
XJ637 U	15.3.57	4.1.61	2 Sqn.
XJ638 D	2.7.57	12.1.61	5 MU
XJ639 C	22.3.57	4.1.61	2 Sqn.
XJ640 T	12.3.57	4.1.61	5 MU
XJ674 A	19.3.57	11.6.58	26 Sqn.

14 Sqn.
XE530	9.5.58	9.6.58	26 Sqn.
XF417	9.5.58	9.6.58	26 Sqn.
XG131 N	7.6.57	7.3.63	19 MU
XG166 K	29.7.57	17.12.62	19 MU
XG210 A	9.4.57	17.2.58	HAL
XG251 E	21.9.59	17.12.62	5 MU
XG274 P	?	?	229 OCU
XG291 O	1.5.57	17.12.62	5 MU
XG292 R	1.5.57	9.6.58	26 Sqn.
XG295 S	8.4.57	5.1.61	5 MU
XJ636 S	2.1.61	17.2.62	19 MU
XJ642 A	8.4.57	17.12.62	19 MU
XJ643 B	8.4.57	22.8.57	Cat.4 HSA
XJ644 C	9.4.57	17.12.62	19 MU
XJ646 D	15.4.57	17.12.62	19 MU
XJ673 E	15.4.57	18.8.59	Cat.4 HSA
XJ689 F	1.5.57	17.12.62	19 MU

XJ690 H	8.5.57	17.12.62	5 MU
XJ691 M	1.5.57	17.12.62	19 MU
XJ695 L	?	?	?
XJ712 B	2.1.61	14.2.63	1 Sqn.

possibly earlier coded L
XJ713 B	2.1.61	?	1 Sqn.

also reported coded G
XJ717 R	12.1.61	14.2.62	54 Sqn
XK149 T	?	?	1 Sqn.

20 Sqn.
XE535 D	27.1.58	11.6.58	26 Sqn.
XG128 Y	?	?	?
XG293 D	?	?	?
XJ680 A	3.5.57	3.1.61	HSA
XJ684 B	3.5.57	3.1.61	HSA
XJ685 C	6.5.57	31.1.61	HSA
XJ686 D	3.5.57	31.1.61	HSA
XJ688 E	3.5.57	9.6.58	26 Sqn.
XJ692 X	5.6.57	31.1.61	HSA
XJ693 W	13.6.57	3.10.60	Cat.5
XJ695 U	31.5.57	7.2.61	14 Sqn
XJ712 F	31.5.57	2.1.61	14 Sqn.

earlier reported coded J
XJ713 G	20.5.57	2.1.61	14 Sqn.
XJ716 T	31.5.57	4.1.61	19 MU
XJ717 Z	31.5.57	9.6.58	26 Sqn.
XK137 V	17.6.57	3.1.61	HSA
XK138 Y	24.6.57	3.1.61	HSA

26 Sqn.
XE530 A	9.6.58	1.2.61	HSA
XE535 F	11.6.58	3.2.61	HSA
XE546 M	18.6.58	?	HSA
XF415 J	9.4.59	4.1.61	19 MU
XF417 B	9.6.58	4.1.61	19 MU
XG208 J	11.6.58	24.3.59	Cat.5
XG292 D	9.6.58	?.1.61	HSA
XG293 G	11.6.58	2.2.61	HSA
XJ632 H	3.7.58	30.1.61	HSA
XJ636 K	24.7.58	2.1.61	14 Sqn.
XJ674 L	11.6.58	11.1.61	5 MU
XJ688 E	9.6.58	31.1.61	HSA
XJ717 Z	9.6.58	12.1.61	14 Sqn.

Hunter FR.10 XF436 'E' of 4 Sqn in 1969, showing to advantage the main differences to the F.6: nose housing three F95 cameras, UHF aerial aft of the cockpit, brake parachute housing above the tailpipe, 'towel rail' aerial for the Marconi radio compass, and 230 gal. long range tanks on the inboard pylons. (Günther Kipp)

93 Sqn.

XE546 Z	29.1.58	18.6.58	26 Sqn.
XE550 R	12.2.58	3.1.61	HSA
XE590	4.6.58	10.7.58	4 Sqn.
XF423	8.3.60	17.1.61	19 MU
XG208 C	9.4.57	11.6.58	26 Sqn.
XG257 C	1.1.60	4.1.61	5 MU
XG258 B	8.4.57	17.5.57	Cat.5
XG272 A	2.4.57	4.1.61	HSA
XG289 Z	29.3.57	29.11.57	Cat.5
XG294 W	22.3.57	1.1.61	2 Sqn.
XG296 X	19.3.57	3.1.61	HSA
XJ632 H	22.3.57	3.7.58	26 Sqn.
XJ633 T	26.3.57	1.5.57	Cat.4
XJ634 V	?	?	229 OCU
XJ635 F	29.3.57	4.1.61	5 MU
XJ641 G	2.4.57	11.11.59	Cat.5
XJ645 E	29.3.57	1.1.61	2 Sqn.
XJ675 T	22.3.57	8.1.60	Cat.5
XJ676 S	?	4.1.61	2 Sqn.
XJ683 D	?	?	HSA
XJ718 B	29.5.57	5.1.61	5 MU

Jever Station Flight

XE590	21.5.58	4.6.58	93 Sqn.

Laarbruch Station Flight

During the temporary grounding of the Buccaneers the following Hunter F.6s ex- 4.FTS were operated as a stop gap, together with T.7/T.8s from approximately May to October 1980, when they went to 5 MU:

XF386
XF526
XF527
XG290

HUNTER T.7s

WV318	6.71	15 Sqn.Laarbruch
	11.77	237 OCU
	? 80/81	Laarbruch S/F *
WV372	12.62	Gütersloh S/F, asTR, 2 Sqn.
	5.67	
	30.3.71	RAE
WV383	6.1.60	79 Sqn.
	8.1.60	Gütersloh S/F
	14.4.61	Jever S/F
	16.5.61	4 Sqn.
	5.6.61	19 MU
XF310 ^	? 80/81	Laarbruch S/F*
XF995 ^	?	Laarbruch S/F*
XL566	? 80/81	Laarbruch S/F*
XL567	? 80/81	Laarbruch S/F*
XL568	?	Laarbruch S/F*
XL573	?	Laarbruch S/F*
XL587	? 80/81	Laarbruch S/F*
XL596	4.6.70	Harrier CU,as 1
	25.8.70	4 Sqn.(Harriers)
XL597	3.11.70	4 Sqn.(Harriers)
	23.4.70	20 Sqn.(Harriers)
XL600	?	Laarbruch S/F*

XL612	19.3.59	APS Sylt
	9.6.61	19 MU
XL613	?	Laarbruch S/F*
XL614	4.5.59	APS Sylt
	8.9.61	19 MU
XL616	1.5.59	APS Sylt
	6.9.61	19 MU
	3.2.66	19 Sqn.(Lightnings)
	20.4.66	5 MU
XL617	?	Laarbruch S/F*
	?	4 Sqn.
	?	Jever S/F
	?	GüterslohS/F
XL618	?	14 Sqn.
XL619	12.5.59	2 TAF
	13.5.59	20 Sqn.
	1.1.61	14 Sqn.
	29.3.61	19 MU
XL621	?	Gütersloh S/F as CL/ 4 Sqn.
	?	
XL622	18.6.59	93 Sqn. as J
	1.1.61	Jever S/F
	7.4.61	Sylt S/F
	18.8.61	5 MU
XL623	?	92 Sqn.(Lightnings)
	?	19 Sqn.(Lightnings)

* Some at least of these aircraft were assigned to Laarbruch in Spring 1980 to maintain flying experience during the temporary grounding of the Buccaneers of Nos.15 and 16 Sqns. A mix of T.7s, T.7As, and T.8s were involved.
^ = known T.8s

Hunter FR.10 XF432 'S' of 2 Sqn at Gütersloh was the personal mount of the C.O., Sqn Ldr R.J.M. David in February '69. Note the duplication of squadron markings beneath the nose door code letter. (via E.Westersotebier)

HUNTER FR.10s

2 Sqn.

	Arr.	Dep.	
WW593 Y	13.1.70		
WW596 N	8.8.61	14.3.66	229 OCU
N	9.5.67		
XE556 W	9.11.61		
XE585 E	27.5.70		
XE605 O	10.2.67		
XE621 H	8.2.61	30.2.62	Cat.5
XE625 I	28.2.61	12.2.70	4 Sqn.
XF422 M	30.6.67	20.12.67	229 OCU
XF428	20.7.65	?	later to HSA
XF432 S	9.2.61	29.1.70	4 Sqn.
XF441 O	27.3.61	20.12.63	1417 Flt.
N	13.3.66	13.3.66	8 Sqn.
XF457 A	15.3.61		later codedT
	26.2.70		4 Sqn.
XF458 W	22.3.61	1.9.65	4 Sqn.
I	11.5.66	17.5.71	HSA
XF459 T	22.2.70	2.3.71	HSA
XG127 Y	?	10.6.68	HSA
XG168 N	28.2.61	1.9.62	19 MU
V	18.11.66	22.5.70	229 OCU
XJ633 S	29.1.70	2.3.71	HSA
XJ694 Z	9.9.63	30.9.63	4 Sqn.

this aircraft was continuously pooled between 2 and 4 Sqns. until 16.2.71 when it departed for HSA.

4 Sqn.

	Arr.	Dep.	
WW593 X	25.2.65	13.1.70	2 Sqn.
WW595 G	3.2.61	?	
XE580 D	25.1.61	4.6.70	HSA
XE585 A	5.1.61	27.5.70	HSA
XE625 F	12.2.70	4.6.70	HSA
XE626 E	25.1.61	?	
U	6.12.66	18.5.70	229 OCU
XF428 C	25.1.61	20.7.65	2 Sqn.
XF432 K	29.1.70	17.5.71	HSA
XF438 E	21.2.61	3.6.70	HSA
XF458 J	1.9.65	11.5.66	2 Sqn.
XF459 F	3.2.61	22.2.70	2 Sqn.
XJ633 H	3.2.61	? '66	recoded K
K	29.1.70		2 Sqn.
XJ694 Z	12.8.63		

thereafter regularly alternated between 2 and 4 Sqns. until its departure to HSA on 16.2.71.

Though superficially almost identical in external appearance, the Hunter F.6 with it's more powerful Avon 203 engine had a significantly better performance in 'clean' configuration without drop tanks than the earlier F.4. These photographs, taken by Heiko Weichardt, and each depicting aircraft coded 'G' of 20 Sqn at Oldenburg make an interesting comparison.

(Upper) F.4 WV390 taxying back to dispersal in November 1956 displays the wide track main undercarriage that gave the Hunter an advantage over it's predecessor, the Sabre 4, as it allowed safe landings even under difficult crosswind conditions. Note the slightly upswept fuselage and smaller diameter jet pipe by comparison with the F.6.

(Lower) F.6 XJ713 in August 1957 with blackened gunports as evidence of an air-to-ground firing sortie.

Hunter FR.10 XF428 'C', 4 Sqn. (Günther Kipp)

Performance Data*

Aircraft Type	Hunter 4		Hunter 6	
Engine	Rolls-Royce Avon 115, 121		Rolls-Royce Avon 203	
Maximum Thrust	3,400 kp	7,500 lb	4,535 kp	10,000 lb
Internal Fuel	1,863 litres	410 Imp gal	1,773 litres	390 Imp gal
Clean Take-off Weight	7,710 kg	17,000 lb	7,891 kg	17,400 lb
Max Speed (at 13,720 m/ 45,000 ft)	967 km/hr	522 knots	976 km/hr	527 knots
Rate of Climb (at 13,720 m/45,000 ft)	5,08 m/sec	1,000 ft/min	8,64 m/sec	1,700 ft/min
Service Ceiling	13,720 m	45,000 ft	14,480 m	47,500 ft
Time to 13.720 m/ 45,000 ft	12,5 min		7,1 min	
Take-off Run to 50 ft/15 m	1,555 m	5,100 ft	1,189 m	3,900 ft

* Performance data of Hunter T 7 and Hunter FR 10 are similar to those of Hunter 4 and Hunter 6 respectively

Accidents involving German-based Hunters

Between 1955 and 1980 a total of 36 German-based Hunters were involved in serious accidents, mostly during flying operations, and usually resulting in the aircraft being written-off. Hunter F.4's were involved in 22 of these accidents, reflecting the rapid introduction of this new high performance fighter at a time when the majority of squadron pilots were in their early twenties and inexperienced.

Alan Pollock was a typical young pilot of that era, and gives the following insight to the spectrum of flying activities and the associated workload to which he and his contemporaries were thrust as a first tourist on an operational Hunter squadron in Germany in the mid-1950's:

"The learning curve of new squadron pilots from the OCU was much helped in the 2TAF flying operational environment, where absolutely anything and everything outside an airway was fair game to prey on, from the moment a pair's wheels went up, as the Leader and Two turned away into wide battle formation. If one hung around and was in touch with the programme planning, it was often possible to scrounge a spare singleton, which might come up without

being planned. This would help a young pilot to become steeped in the various tactics of flying 1v1, 1v2, 1v4, as opposed to the regular diet of 2v4, 4v6, 4v8 etc, with or without the quite proficient 2TAF Sector GCI.

The range of operational flying tasks and skills to be acquired was quite formidable, and included the following, to mention but a few: Intuitive judgement of distances to defensive breaks or hard turns, offensive feint attacks, dissimilar aircraft fighting, every aspect of dog-fighting and station-keeping in the horizontal or vertical, cine tail-chasing, low level battle and navigation, aerobatics, practice

(Above) The tail of Hunter F.6 XJ675 'T' of 93 Sqn on the roof of a house in Middels, near Aurich, Germany, which crashed on 8 January 1960 after an engine flame-out while being flown by the C.O., Sqn Ldr D. S. White, who ejected safely.
(Below) The same aircraft being lifted by the salvage crew. (Norbert Giese)

diversions, rapid recoveries or paired QGH descents into stepped down ACR7 or full GCA talkdowns ...all of which could be accomplished by persistent exposure to the widest possible exploration of the Hunter's forgiving handling envelope, and our training syllabus. When viewed in context with this most demanding repertoire of operational training tasks the 2TAF Hunter accident rates were quite remarkable."

(Above) Hunter F.6 XG270 'D' of 4 Sqn being dismantled after an emergency landing on the mud flats south of the North Sea island of Baltrum on 31 May 1957, caused by engine failure. Its pilot, Flt Sgt T.E.(Ginger) Ratcliffe, survived unhurt, only to be killed while flying a 4 Sqn Hunter FR.10 on 24 January 1967. XG270 had to be written off as it was swamped by the in-coming tide before it could be moved to higher ground which was unfortunate because it had only been delivered to the squadron on 28 February and was virtually brand new with few airframe hours. (J.Harms)

(Right, upper and centre) The sad remains of Hunter 4 WT714 'F' of 14 Sqn the first of the type to be lost in 2TAF when it crashed 3 miles from Bassum near Bremen on 18 August 1955 killing the pilot Fg Off William Deluce, 24, after a mid air collision with another 14 Sqn F.4, WT807 whose 22 year old pilot, Sgt P.M. Stone ejected safely. (Roger Lindsay collection)

(Lower right) Hunter F.4 XF932 'A', the C.O.'s aircraft of 234 Sqn crashed on 22 September 1956 after suffering a fire on take-off from Kleine Brogel airfield, Belgium.
(Roger Lindsay collection)

Accidents involving German-based Hunters

Type	Serial	Unit	Date	Home Base	Detail
Hunter 4	WT714	14 Sqn	18.8.55	Oldenburg	Collision with WT 807 near Bremen killing Fg Off W. Deluce
Hunter 4	WT738	118 Sqn	20.10.55	Jever	Collided with WT 757 west of Hamburg while engaged in high altitude cine' exercise. Both pilots left their aircraft, but neither survived. Pilot of this aircraft was Fg Off B. L.Rogers
Hunter 4	WT743	118 Sqn	3.57	Jever	Damaged by acid from burst battery and declared Cat. 4 at 71 MU Bicester. Sold for scrap to S.S. Coley 1.1.59
Hunter 4	WT757	118 Sqn	20.10.55	Jever	Collided with WT 738; pilot, Fg Off John McLennan, was killed
Hunter 4	WT799	4 Sqn	6.3.56	Jever	Damaged in wheels-up landing; declared Cat. 4, to Hawker Aircraft 24.9.57. To Admiralty 6.2.59.
Hunter 4	WT806	14 Sqn	17.6.55	Oldenburg	Aircraft overstressed in tight turn: pilot o.k., repaired by Hawker Aircraft. To 5 MU Kemble, later issued to CFS Little Rissington. To Admiralty 21.7.61
Hunter 4	WT807	14 Sqn	18.8.55	Oldenburg	Collision with WT 714; pilot, Sergeant P.M. Stone, o.k.
Hunter 4	WV257	26 Sqn	22.7.55	Oldenburg	Stalled on landing at Oldenburg, destroying runway caravan and two fire tenders, pilot o.k to Admiralty 19.10.61
Hunter 4	WV261	26 Sqn	13.1.56	Oldenburg	Crash landing; later GIA 7780M at Halton
Hunter 4	WV271	4 Sqn	23.10.55	Jever	Crashed during beat-up of Oldenburg airfield; pilot, Sergeant E. H. Williams killed
Hunter 4	WV274	118 Sqn	16.7.57	Jever	Damaged as result of forced landing when engine failed during an attempted overshoot
Hunter 4	WV373	118 Sqn	8.12.55	Jever	Accident happened at Ahlhorn; after three GCAs in manual control pilot reverted to powered control and apparently obtained false anchorage of the ailerons. This only allowed free movement in one direction with consequential loss of control. Pilot, Fg Off A. R. J. Yoemans, was killed after he jettisoned canopy but failed to eject
Hunter 4	WV384	71 Sqn	5.4.57	Brüggen	Engine failed on approach; pilot, Fg Off A. Shucksmith, was killed, when he ejected but seat did not operate properly
Hunter 4	WV395	20 Sqn	11.3.57	Oldenburg	Fire in the air but landed successfully, declared Cat. 4 and eventually used for ground instruction at Cosford
Hunter 4	WV412	112 Sqn	13.9.56	Brüggen	Aircraft crashed due to engine flame-out on approach to Sylt when pilot, Flt Lt K. A. Williamson, successfully ejected at 800ft, landed in water but was later picked up by helicopter
Hunter 4	WW664	26 Sqn	25.5.56	Oldenburg	Aircraft damaged in crash-landing after engine flame-out at Ahlhorn and suffered Cat. 3 damage. Pilot, Flt Lt N. J. R. Walpole, unhurt. Repaired at Hawker Aircraft and to Admiralty 30.3.58.
Hunter 4	XE669	98 Sqn	4.12.56	Jever	Aircraft crashed due to engine fire just after take-off when jet pipe had worked loose and after pilot, Fg Off D. J.Young, ejected. In the event he did not separate from the seat and was killed - subsequently it was discovered, that the barostat had been incorrectly fitted, and this had prevented automatic separation
Hunter 4	XF290	67 Sqn	14.8.56	Brüggen	Aircraft crashed due to engine failure during take-off; pilot, Lieutenant M. V. Maina, RN, ejected and landed unhurt
Hunter 4	XF305	67 Sqn	28.11.56	Brüggen	Aircraft destroyed by fire on ground at Sylt on start-up when two starter cartridges were fired simultaneously
Hunter 4	XF932	234 Sqn	22.9.56	G'kirchen	Aircraft crashed after fire on take-off at Kleine-Brogel
Hunter 4	XF945	234 Sqn	20.11.56	G'kirchen	Aircraft crashed due to engine flame-out 15 miles south east of Aachen. Pilot, Fg Off P A Marsh, tried unsuccessfully to relight engine and ejected, sustaining minor injuries.

Type	Serial	Unit	Date	Home Base	Details
Hunter 4	XF949	3 Sqn	11.1.57	G'kirchen	Aircraft destroyed by fire due to two cartridges firing when starting the engine
Hunter 6	XE590	4 Sqn	9.11.60	Jever	Crashed due to bird strikes near Jever; pilot o.k.
Hunter 6	XG208	26 Sqn	24.3.59	Gütersloh	Crashed three miles west of Gütersloh after being abandoned due to loss of engine power. Pilot, Flt. Lt. R.V. Boult, ejected safely
Hunter 6	XG258	93 Sqn	17.5.57	Jever	Crashed while practising with aerobatic-team at Spangdahlem after bomburst; pilot, Flt Lt B. A. Sanderson, was killed
Hunter 6	XG270	4 Sqn	31.5.57	Jever	Force-landed after engine flame-out, due to explosion in engine bay, on mud flats south of the island of Baltrum. Despite efforts by local people to tow it to higher ground, the rising tide swamped the aircraft, which resulted in a write-off. Pilot, Flt Sergeant T.L. Ratcliffe safe
Hunter 6	XG289	93 Sqn	29.10.57	Jever	Crashed 1 1/2 miles north east of Sylt, after hydraulic power failure on take-off. Unable to stop, the aircraft overshot the airfield into trees. Pilot safe
Hunter 6	XG295	14 Sqn	11.5.57	Oldenburg	Collided with XJ 643 but aircraft repaired, pilot o.k.
Hunter 6	XJ641	93 Sqn	11.11.59	Jever	Crashed at night into sea off Dutch coast; pilot took off from Jever despite poor radio reception and had frequent problems with radio communications until all contact was lost. No trace of pilot, Fg Off R. M. West, or aircraft
Hunter 6	XJ643	14 Sqn	11.5.57	Oldenburg	Collided with XG 295 but aircraft repaired, pilot o.k.
Hunter 6	XJ675	93 Sqn	8.1.60	Jever	Aircraft crashed after engine flame-out near Aurich, pilot, Sqn Ldr D. S. White ejected unhurt
Hunter 6	XJ693	20 Sqn	3.10.60	Gütersloh	Written off after wheels-up landing due to undercarriage jamming in "up" position, Pilot safe
Hunter FR 10	WW595	4 Sqn	24.1.67	Gütersloh	Aircraft crashed into hill near Fürstenberg/Weser, Tragically Master Pilot T. L. Ratcliffe, who had survived forced landing in Hunter 6 XG 270 of 4 Sqn, Jever, on 31.5.57, was killed
Hunter FR 10	XE621	2 Sqn	30.1.62	Gütersloh	Aircraft stalled and dived into the ground near Papenburg; the pilot, Flt Lt C. B. Barnes, was killed
Hunter FR 10	XF422	2 Sqn	11.3.67	Gütersloh	Aircraft hit high tension cables during sortie from Stavanger-Sola in Norway, sustaining major damage to main plane. Flt Lt F. Mitchell remained unhurt and managed to land aircraft. After re-purchase by manufacturer, aircraft was converted to Singaporean Hunter FR74 B

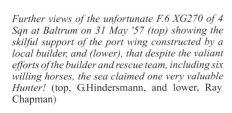

Further views of the unfortunate F.6 XG270 of 4 Sqn at Baltrum on 31 May '57 (top) showing the skilful support of the port wing constructed by a local builder, and (lower), that despite the valiant efforts of the builder and rescue team, including six willing horses, the sea claimed one very valuable Hunter! (top, G.Hindersmann, and lower, Ray Chapman)

At The Sharp End:
Pilots' Recollections

'Bugs' Bendell *(67 & 4 Sqns.)*

After I had been on 67 Squadron for about four months, Flt. Lt. Lee Jones, one of the Flight Commanders on 112 Squadron who had recently graduated from the Fighter Leaders School at West Raynham, was authorised to lead a sweep, commonly known as a 'wing Ding', against the USAFE fighter squadrons in 4ATAF. It was quite usual for the Brüggen squadrons to operate as a wing; we conformed to the same standard operating procedures or SOPs, as they were called, and we were often tasked as a wing during major exercises. But this time it was different: Lee had telephoned the USAFE base at Bitburg and had thrown down the gauntlet, so to speak, telling them that the Brüggen wing would be overhead at 1500 hrs, and that they - the USAFE - could do nothing about it. Needless to say, the Yanks had other ideas 'Who is this crazy Limey anyway?' and they made plans.

The Brüggen squadrons eventually produced twenty-four aircraft. I was programmed to fly as Blue Four - the last aircraft in the formation - but at least I had been selected for the home team, which I took as a compliment.

The weather was perfect, eight eighths blue - not a cloud in the sky. The start-up and radio checks went without a hitch:

'Gold, check in.' 'Two. Three. Four' and so on, until the twenty-four Hunters were lined up on the runway. It was hot and turbulent at the back end during the

engine checks. At last we were ready for take-off, in pairs at five-second intervals: the first pair pulled high, the next stayed low, the next high, and so on. In that way successive pairs avoided the turbulent wake of the aircraft ahead. Lee Jones climbed in a wide spiral to allow Brüggen Combine to join up.

Contrails started at 25,000 ft; from the briefing we knew that they would be persistent above this altitude. The Americans could see us coming almost from the top of the climb, but for fuel conservation we had to stay high, as the Hunter F.4's radius of action was limited. Brüggen Combine made a brave sight, though, as it headed south.

About twenty miles from Brüggen, a lone Meteor F.8 crossed our path and in clipped R/T, Lee directed Blue Three and Four to take care of the bogey at eleven o'clock low. My adrenaline started pumping; this was going to be exciting. The Meteor was certainly no threat to Brüggen Combine, but one never

Straight at the photographer... this Hunter 6 XJ632 'H' of 26 Sqn with everything down gives a good idea of the wide track main undercarriage which was helpful in crosswind landings. The large flaps and the absence of fins on the 100 gal drop tanks are also evident in this view. (D.Schmidt)

questioned the leader. Our bogey was probably a Belgian Air Force Meteor; at least, he was heading in that direction, but the pilot had seen what was going on and had wisely decided to run for cover. We chased him but he had too much of a head start and he disappeared in the industrial haze at low level, north of the Ardennes.

We climbed back up to high level, hoping to rejoin Brüggen Combine, but they were long gone. Instead we found a geriatric USAF B-45 bomber, cruising sedately by at 15,000 ft. It would have been churlish to ignore him, so we each made a quarter attack and took gun

67 Sqn Hunter F.4 WV367 setting out on a sortie from Brüggen early in 1956 prior to it being coded 'X' (via Peter Caygill).

camera film to back up our 'splash' claim - that was the simulated destruction of the B-45. Then we set course for home. We were the first pair to land, but the rest of Brüggen Combine was not far behind. Jones called for the debriefing In 112 Squadron's crew-room. He opened the proceedings by asking the members of the formation to state their claims. There was a painful silence, then the whole of Brüggen Combine, to a man, announced, 'I got a B-45.' We were all claiming the same aircraft.

Then the sorry tale unfolded. Following Lee's phone challenge, Bitburg had called for assistance from the other USAFE bases; someone had spoken to the Canadians who were always game for a scrap - and they had roped in one or two French squadrons. As for Brüggen Combine, after Blue Three and Four had left, Lee had continued to fritter away sections of the formation: a pair here to take out a French Air Force Vautour; a pair there to chase four Dutch F-84's, and so on. The only members of Brüggen Combine to arrive overhead Bitburg were Lee Jones and his No.2. They were met by forty plus American, Canadian and French fighters. Lee had been hard pressed to hold the initiative. Fortunately he had a height advantage, and after circling high out of reach for a while, he and his wingman had gone down through the middle of the pack and high-tailed it for home with half of NATO snapping at their heels.

Occasionally an incident occurs in the air that cannot easily be forgotten. On 28 March 1958 I was leading two 4 Squadron Hunter F.6s on a high level battle formation sortie. My official report on what happened reads as follows:

"During the climb I noted that all oxygen indications were satisfactory, the flow was normal and 100 per cent oxygen was selected. Shortly after levelling at 37,000ft we split for air combat and the next thing I remember was regaining consciousness at 7,000 ft. descending, with the throttle closed, air brakes out, and oxygen selected to emergency We continued the sortie below 10,000ft. I made a normal approach and landing at base."

Alan Pollock, my No.2, was able to fill in the details: after too easily gaining the ascendancy in the dogfight and seeing my aircraft roll inverted into a steep dive, Al asked if I was OK. Receiving no R/T reply he immediately suspected anoxia, and using my own name instead of the official call-sign, he instructed me to pull my emergency oxygen supply and re-connect my main tube, which I apparently silently obeyed. Formatting on my wing tip, and flying on instruments through three separate cloud layers Al

'Bugs' Bendall (left) and Alan Pollock beside 4 Sqn. ops. board during a Sylt APC, February 1958, depicting pilots' names, call signs, ciné/live sorties, number and colour of rounds fired and scores (Alan Pollock)

managed to talk us through a controlled descent, until at 8,500 ft. I recovered in an instant, and (he considered rather cheekily) resumed the lead!

I was met at the aircraft by the station medical officer. In the absence of long-term ill effects, it seemed likely that I had been anoxic - probably due to a disconnected oxygen supply. At that time the tube from the pilot's oxygen mask was attached to the aircraft supply by a push-fit connector, which was designed to detach easily during an ejection. Unfortunately the connector could just as easily become disconnected in flight. At high altitude, air is not an adequate substitute for oxygen, but the effects of anoxia are so insidious that a break in the oxygen supply could easily go unnoticed. Fortunately, Al Pollock was on the ball. With that kind of problem. pilots of single-seat aircraft were seldom given a second chance.

Some months later a safety valve was fitted to the oxygen connector which prevented the pilot drawing breath through the mask when the tube was disconnected. This modification provided a positive warning of inadvertent oxygen disconnection.

Extracts from Anthony 'Bugs' Bendell's book 'Never in Anger'.

Mike Hall (26 Sqn)

On the morning of 12 August 1955, having recently re-equipped with our new squadron aircraft, Hunter F.4s, we pre-briefed for a four ship sortie... battle formation to operating altitude of 40,000 feet, followed by a cine-gun exercise and ending with a tail-chase. I was to fly number four in the second element. We took off in pairs as Red section and climbed out to the south west of base. On reaching four-zero, the leader called for 'long line astern' and for some ten minutes we carried out manoeuvres with the gun-sight and the gun-camera 'on'. At the end of this phase, Red leader called for 'tail-chase', which was merely an extension of the previous exercise with more emphasis on aerobatics. I elected to switch the gun-camera and gun-sight off and concentrate on maintaining my tail position in the formation at 100 - 150 yards.

The gun-sight in the Hunter F.4 was, at that time, retractable. This was in order to enhance forward visibility through the windscreen, particularly in the landing pattern. I selected 'Retract'. The operating switch was on the instrument hood immediately to the right of the sight and, on the right-hand side of the sight body was a 'terry-clip', if I remember correctly, to house the radar connection, not then fitted. At the time the aircraft was in a hard 7g right-hand turn as I tried to maintain station on Red 3, so I was forced to use my left hand to operate the switch. Since my arm and hand were also affected by the 'g'-force, it took considerable effort to reach the switch. The gun-sight, operated by a very powerful electrical worm-drive, started to retract, my cape leather glove caught on the radar cable clip and before I could remove my hand, my middle and third fingers became trapped by the clip across the middle joints, dislocating both fingers, forcing back my left wrist to its limit and jamming my elbow over the right-hand side of the control column, causing it to deflect laterally several degrees to the left. I was also twisted to the right against the seat restraining harness, and thus, immobilised in a massive 'mechanical lock'.

The aircraft, now in a 20 degree port descending turn, commenced to roll further to the left. Unable to use the stick to correct it, I instinctively applied right rudder. This effectively stopped the roll but left the aircraft flying left wing low. I stared at my hand in horrified disbelief I tried to push my fingers further forward, in order to 'hook' them round the clip, but I had literally stalled the electrical drive and the gun-sight just sank lower as the pain level shrieked upwards. 'Christ, you silly bugger, now what are you going to do?' I thought. 'How the hell am I going to get this thing back to base let alone land it? I'm going to have to bale out. Damn it, that's not an option.. if I eject, I shall tear my arm off and even if I survive ejection, I'll probably bleed to death before they get to me. I've no option but to ride it down!' I struggled to stop rising panic.. .I needed to take stock of the wider situation. Apart from the induced roll to the left, what else needed my attention? I was effectively denied the use of anything on the left-hand side of the cockpit, flaps and undercarriage levers on the instrument panel; air-brakes and R/T button on the throttle lever and engine re-light button on the HP cock, the only control near at hand. 'God-Almighty! How the bloody hell was I going to fly this thing?' I felt the icy clamp of stark terror grip my mind ... I had to do something to combat it.

All this had taken but a few vital seconds and, to my surprise, I was still more or less in the formation. I had to reach the R/T button! I was using my right hand to force the stick as close to the central position as possible and I would have to release my grip, cross over my left arm and try for the button. I tried, failed and the aircraft rolled over to 110 degrees as I desperately kicked on top rudder and grabbed the stick. At all costs I had to get her nose up. If it dropped there was no way that I would ever get it level again. 'Loosen off the seat restraining harness!' I slackened the shoulder straps as the aircraft rolled onto its back. Against the pain I jammed the stick over to the right and slowly she righted herself, but I still had to let someone know what was going down. I tried for the R/T button again and with the shoulder straps slackened, succeeded.. .with the tip of my middle finger.. .just!

'*Red 3 from Red 4 over.*'

'*Red 4, Red 3, go-ahead?*'

The aircraft rolled again. It was easier to let it roll and I caught it as it came up level.

'*I have two fingers trapped in the gun-sight over.*'

'*Red 4, say again!!!*'

'*Red 3.. .I have my left hand trapped in the gun-sight!*'

The aircraft executed two rolls and I caught it as it came up level, second time around.

'*Roger Red 4, Red 3 copied. Have you tried re-selecting the sight?*'

'*Affirmative.. .no joy, the motor's stalled.. .just gone further down!*'.

With loosened straps I could get more top rudder and succeeded in holding the roll down to a steep bank. My middle finger was now bent almost double backwards and the third finger was at 45 degrees. The geometric lock I was in tightened its grip and I blacked out. Vaguely I heard Red 3 calling. The aircraft rolled at least twice before I managed to regain control.

'*Red 3... I keep blacking out!*'

Red 3's aircraft moved in closer and I could see Peter clearly now. He couldn't do much, but it made a hell of a difference! Red 4 copied. Try to concentrate.

'*Don't transmit unless you have to. Break/break. Oldenburg tower this is Red 3. Red 4 has fingers trapped in gun-sight. Unable to remove. Our position is three zero miles south west at 33,000 feet. We are RTB.*'

'*Red 3 from tower, we copy. Steer 030. Over*'

'*Red 3, Roger. Out*'

'*Red 3, Red 4, I'm descending to 20,000 Feet*'

'*Red 3 Roger. I'll keep transmitting to you. Keep awake! Hang in there!*'

'*Red 4 from Oldenburg tower. Stand by whilst we get technical information on the sight. Over*'

An oil painting by Bruno Albers in 1956 of Oldenburg's 26 Sqn aerobatic team is portrayed diving out of a loop, set against a dramatic skyscape that year. The team was led by Flt Lt Geoff Wilkinson. (Bruno Albers)

'*This is Red 4.. .negative on that! No time. I'm coming in. Forced landing pattern from two zero. Out!*' '*Red 4 this is tower, understood. Break/break all Oldenburg traffic keep clear of the circuit. We have an emergency. Out*'

I needed 20 degrees of flap, air-brakes and undercarriage down. The air brake switch, on the throttle, close to the R/T button, was just reachable, but the flap lever was on the left of the instrument panel and the undercarriage selector was there too, but even further to the left. I loosened off the shoulder straps completely. I was now committed to staying on board.

The aircraft was now in a descending port turn and at all costs, I had to try and prevent it rolling further left. I stood hard on the left rudder pedal and wrenched myself across the cockpit and succeeded in selecting flaps. The flap lever gave two clicks (20 degrees). I grabbed the stick and corrected the roll! Under-cart! Up or down? Belly landing? No.. .it had to be wheels! I struggled to reach the undercarriage lever. Finally after several attempts, flailing my arm wildly, the middle finger of my right hand made contact with it and there was a satisfying rumble from the undercart. Once more I collared the stick and

struggled to combat the increasing roll to the left. The indicator lights changed to 'red' and one by one changed to 'green'. I heaved a mental sigh of relief, now I only needed to concentrate on maintaining a left-hand descending turn at 250 knots and set up for a forced Landing. Thank God there wasn't much cloud about and the visibility was good. I could see base below. Maybe I was going to make it down after all!!' I continued the descent and entered the downwind circuit pattern at 2,000 feet. I still had limited fingertip control over the throttle, but I'd checked the limit of my control of power at 20,000 feet and although I'd managed to set it for the descent, all I would have for landing was full power or idle... no intermediate power settings! This was going to have to be a one shot attempt and it had to be right!

I turned on to Finals and checked 'Three Greens'. The fields on the approach swept by below. Dear God, I'm too low.. .too slow.. .down to 130 knots! I need power.. .Now! I was 300 yards in the undershoot and I had to let go the stick! Christ! The starboard wing swung up to 60 degrees and the engine went to full power. The aircraft gave a gut-wrenching surge and streaked the remaining distance to the runway threshold. I grabbed the stick and tried to level her. Now the speed was increasing at an alarming rate and the aircraft was climbing away! I had to close the throttle.. .I dare not attempt a 'Go- Around'.. .I didn't have the strength left. I hesitated.. .the aircraft was still not level. 'Christ man! Do it.. .DO IT!' For the last time, I let go and smashed the throttle lever shut. 175 knots! The starboard wing was well over 90 degrees and I saw the direction numbers painted on the runway flash above the port wing-tip as it 'scraped' mere inches above the centre-line. I grabbed the control column and wrenched it over to the right. After what seemed a life time, the aircraft started to right itself. The port wheel hit the runway and I grabbed a handful of brakes. The left anti-skid system operated, but the right wheel, still clear of the tarmac, locked up. . . slammed on to the runway and the tyre exploded with a monstrous bang! The aircraft veered off in a searing right turn and left the runway. The starboard undercarriage dug in and she swung through 120 degrees and stopped. With some difficulty, I shut down the engine and opened the canopy. The fresh air had never smelt so sweet! I looked out to the runway threshold; to my astonishment, I was barely 400 yards from it! Normal threshold speed for the Hunter was 130-135 knots. I had landed at 175 knots and probably achieved the shortest landing run on record! I was astonished to see a great sea of faces, half the entire station personnel seemed to be out there on the grass and perimeter track! Someone brought out an inspection ladder. The sortie had lasted 45 minutes.. .it took another 15 or 20 minutes for the ground crew to try and extract me from the cockpit, during which time the MO was filling me full of morphine which had no effect whatsoever! In the end I 'borrowed' a pair of pliers from one of the engineers and tore off the offending terry- clip! Apart from this and the burst tyre,

miraculously the aircraft had suffered no damage. Even the sight motor was still operative! By some miracle, it had not caused an electrical fire! I was carted off to the nearby Royal Air Force hospital at Rostrup. The fingers looked grotesque... like two bent cricket bats! Much to my surprise, apart from a chipped knuckle on the middle finger they were not badly damaged. The third finger straightened up after about ten days, but the middle finger remained bent at about ten degrees forward. Following this incident, I gained somewhat dubious fame... the gun sight installation was modified. The retraction facility was deleted and the sight set in an intermediate position lowered from its previous height when fully extended! Some thirty years later, long after I had left the Air Force, there was a sharp crack one day and the finger returned to normal! Had it not been for Pete Perry, my element leader, who was there when I needed him during those first horrifying minutes, had the weather been less than fair and had the gods not been with me that day, I doubt whether this tale would have been written!

(Above) A sketch by Mike Hall entitled 'Hairy Approach' depicting the most frightening moment of his ordeal on 12 August 1955
(Below) the Green Endorsement (so called because they were originally written in green ink) he subsequently received from Air Vice Marshall P.N. Ubee (AOC 2 Group) which read:

Instances of avoidance by Exceptional flying Skill and Judgement of Loss of, or Damage to, Aircraft or Personnel.

On 12th August 1955, Flying Officer Hall, whilst flying at 40,000 feet in Hunter WW664 had two fingers of his left hand trapped by the retracting gunsight. Unable to free his hand, and suffering considerable pain he landed his aircraft safely back at base. At the time he had 23:10 hours on Hunters. Throughout, Hall remained calm and displayed a high standard of airmanship in very difficult circumstances.

Pilots and ground crews of the newly reformed 26 Sqn at Ahlhorn, summer 1958, in front of F.6 XE535 'F'. (Mike Hall, who is third from the left, front row)

Alan East *(3 Sqn.)*

Alan had flown Sabre F 4s with 3 Sqn. for two years, and was a section leader with more than 260 hours on the type by the time the squadron converted to Hunter F 4s in the summer of 1956.

Sometime in early 1956 Flt.Lt. Chas Boyer left No. 2(AC) Squadron, which shares a birth date with No.3(F) Sqn. and which were also then at Geilenkirchen, to do the Day Fighter Leader School (DFLS) course at West Raynham. This was done on Hunters. Then in May, I think, Charles was posted to No.3(F) Sqn. both as 'A' Flt. Commander and to organise the conversion to the Hunter F.4. He produced the posters and gave the lectures and briefings. There were no 2-seat Hunters at that time but there had never been a 2-seat RAF Sabre either, so it was no big deal to have somebody sit on the ladder for your first engine start and maybe the first attempt at taxying - and then you were on your own! My first Hunter flight was 35 minutes on 3 July 1956.

There was a lot of natural loyalty to the Sabre, especially among the pilots who had trained in the US. Remember that in the early 1950s, because of the Korean War, the RAF had expanded at such a rate that many of its aircrew had to be trained in the US, Canada or Southern Rhodesia. I went to Canada. So poor Charles faced a fair bit of flak, mostly good humoured, some of it serious, but probably none of it justified. We complained about the retrograde step of losing the Sabre's radar gun sight to the model familiar from training on Vampire or Meteor - conveniently forgetting the poor performance of the Sabre sight in the early days! We feigned to miss the comfort of the Sabre's 'armchair' seat - ignoring the superior performance of the Martin Baker one, and the fact that we no longer had to carry our personal back parachute to and from the aircraft each sortie! We criticised the lack of nose wheel steering, and the hard ride of the Hunter's oleos and high pressure tyres -

not acknowledging the advantage of the Dunlop 'Maxaret' brakes! But it all soon died down and as we became more familiar with the new type we acknowledged its worth. After all, we had only had the Sabre as an interim measure because the Hunter was late coming into service.

Civil airliners were still propeller driven and stayed mainly below 20,000 feet, and as I recall, there was no organised airways system much above that. Something we did frequently was to fly a high level sweep to the south looking for Canadian Sabre 5s and later 6s (both with more powerful Orenda engines) or American F-86Ds or F-86Fs to play with. Their performance had often proved too much for our Sabre 4s with only 5,200 lbs. of static thrust - 2,000 lbs. less than the Sabre 6. We soon learned to appreciate the Hunter's better climb and dog-fighting performance. One of the few valid criticisms of the Hunter was its poorer view, rearward and downward, but that seemed to be the result of the contemporary national design philosophy.

Initially, the turbulence of firing all four guns at once caused an engine compressor surge. It was also bloody

Alan East (then a young Flying Officer) leads a formation in his 3 Sqn Sabre F.4 XB640 'P', followed by a second Sabre XB749 'A', and one of Geilenkirchen's first brand new Hunter F.4s, XF944, as yet without squadron markings or code letter, but in fact already on the strength of 234 Sqn on this date, 24 May 1956, and not, as sometimes suggested, 3 Sqn. (Ron Ledwidge / Günther Kipp)

noisy! We were restricted to firing only two at a time and later an electrical 'fuel Dipping' modification was fitted which, when the trigger was pressed, reduced the fuel flow to match the anticipated reduced airflow into the intake. By September we were back at Sylt enjoying the Hunter's far superior fire power. For some reason I did not record my scores for that detachment, but upon leaving the squadron in April 1957 my gunnery assessment was average! However, I did fly another six sorties flag towing in the Meteor. I also discovered that I could stow my guitar in its case vertically in the electrical bay behind the cockpit. Couldn't do that in a Sabre! We practised low

A Christmas card cartoon by one of 3 Sqn's pilots, Alan Chapman, shows the 'conversion' of a Sabre into a Hunter, such was the eager anticipation of re-equipment with the new Hawker fighter. Realisation proved slightly less sustaining, as many pilots were initially sorry to see the replacement of the Sabres. (Alan Chapman via Alan East /3 Sqn Association)

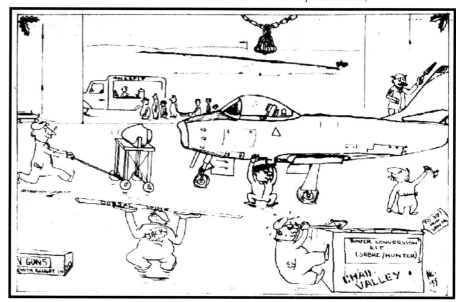

Hunter 4s of 4 Sqn are rarely illustrated, despite having arguably amongst the most striking livery of any 2TAF F.4 squadrons, exemplified by XE667 'Z' photographed at Geilenkirchen on 3 April 1956. (Robin Brown via Andy Thomas)

flying, low level strikes and even a few sorties of cine air-to-ground at Monschau but we do not appear to have done any live air-to-ground firing with Hunters. I do not remember why.

The range was conveniently close by in the Eifel, not far from Geilenkirchen, on higher ground near the Belgian border, which made it a favourite crossing place for those desperate to smuggle such things as coffee into Germany. On earlier occasions while flying Sabres, and viewing our cine films afterwards, we could see figures scurrying in the background, apparently hoping that the border guards would not follow them while we were firing!

My tour on No.3(F) Sqn. finished in April 1957, just a few weeks after all personnel had assembled in the Astra, the Station Cinema, to be addressed by the Station Commander. Duncan Sandys' 1957 Defence White Paper had proposed that the manned fighter was virtually obsolete; its role could be filled by missiles! The Second World War had finished only 12 years earlier. Just half a generation! As the Gp. Capt. read out a long list of squadrons to be disbanded, including our own No.3(F) Sqn. the first in the world ever to be fully equipped with heavier-than-air machines! - most of those wearing medal ribbons were near to tears. The squadron was disbanded on 15 June 1957. Eventually the folly of not keeping alive the identity of the senior low-number squadrons was acknowledged.

Charles Boyack *(4 Sqn.)*

My time on 4 Sqn. Between 1953 and 1956 included flying Vampires, Sabres and finally the Hunter 4, and this tale concerns a chap who had just reached the approved standard of experience on Hunters to take part in Battle Flight operations. In those days squadrons always scrambled five (when possible) to try and guarantee four getting airborne. If all five got off, the spare, No.5, carried out a local training sortie and landed back. On this particular misty morning, as dawn was (nearly) breaking, the first four taxied down to the Battle Flight dispersal at the far end of the field. No.5, our hero, had to wait for a small snag to be cleared. When this was done, he set off for the dispersal after telling the ground crew to leave the ladder plugged in, since he expected to be on stand-by for some time. For the same reason, he didn't bother to do up his straps or remove the 'top pin' (of the ejection seat) although he did plug in the radio lead. He had almost reached the dispersal, when the Verey was fired from the tower to scramble Battle Flight. He frantically took out the 'top pin' and did up his straps, accidentally disconnecting his radio lead in his struggles. He then swung on to the runway in his No.5 position as the others roared off ahead, totally forgetting the ladder. Meanwhile, the runway controller startled by all the excitement and activity, saw the ladder and called, 'last aircraft on Battle Flight, abandon take-off', No.5 was not connected to his radio. No. 4 had not seen No.5 coming up behind him, assumed the call was for him and took prompt, if rather too harsh, action, bursting a tyre in the process, No. 5 was surprised to see the aircraft ahead spearing off the runway with a cloud of smoke, but thought what a good job it was that he had been able to join the scramble. Some 15,000 feet (upwards) later, he managed to get his radio lead connected and was surprised to be told to

maintain steady flight while his aircraft was inspected by the No.3. Fortunately, damage to both aircraft was minimal and there were no complaints received from people on the ground about being strafed with red pieces of metal.

Alan Pollock *(26 & 4 Sqns)*

Alan flew with 26 when it was equipped with F.4s at Oldenburg; following its disbandment he moved to 4 Sqn flying F.6s from Jever, before transferring to 26 after it reformed, also with F.6s; these are some of his memories and observations from those days.

Hunter F.4's surge. Surges were only occasionally experienced but one flew with diligence to avoid both the r.p.m. and thrust vanishing, as one's JPT began to soar. Only diving away with wings level would slowly cure things, meaning the other in this pair having to cover and support a Mk.4, quite quickly found a mile or two below. 'Surge' was usually caused by high angle of attack (as in an emergency break), coupled with over zealous throttle handling or with the 100 series engine's misadjustment. This tendency at altitude was prone to happen to the less experienced guys for more than one reason:

(a) they were invariably the outer ones, who needed to be most agile if a battle break was called towards you, you certainly had to get your own bank, turn and power on smartly for technique, position and flight safety collision avoidance.

(b) The more experienced on the Sqn. would tend to have the choice of their aircraft; some aircraft were more prone and known to be 'surgers' if someone was diving to sort out his surge problem, inevitably the formation's vector flexibility was curtailed, seemingly for a variable time from just 30 seconds to much more. When the big 200 series Rolls-Royce Avon engines in occasional 'surging' would become a distant memory.

Operational ceiling with the F.6 in 1958: 45,000 ft. was realistic to be up in battle fours or, even more memorably, the occasional eight ship formations with even a pair up at 48,000 ft., depending on length of headings and the purpose of the flight, fuel and external tanks, plus the amount of manoeuvring, inevitably affected your best operating height. At times a section was better being lower and faster, depending on the opposition and whether one was with or without GCI assistance or on offensive sweeps - tactics would vary but No.3s (4 outside) would be down-sun so they could scan into sun, normally always having extra height in reserve, as a pair to be able to do their job better. Clean (without drop tanks) and/or in a good aircraft such as No.4 Sqn. Boss' 'A', you could manoeuvre at 50,000 ft. and above.

I only saw the really vivid 'earth's curvature' three or four times. In a Hunter, 54,000ft. was the highest I reached one night, when I did also experience a touch of that 'planet detachment sensation', which some pilots reported. This was with two empty inboards - if punched clean of tanks, surely the Mk. 6 could have struggled up to 56,000 ft. with that welcome 200 series engine, although you were theoretically limited to 48,000 ft. for your own good! Often this 'detachment syndrome' was when executing a finally flapped zoom on a horizon-less pitch black night among the stars, taking advantage of the Hunter's excellent low speed handling 'with nothing on the clock'.

Hunter let-downs - QGH, into ACR 7,

or GCA airfield approaches:

Navigational and bad weather aids in the mid 1950s for jet fighters travelling fast at all altitudes or needing rapid recovery in marginal conditions were primitive compared with later sophisticated facilities, instantly available. While GCI (Ground Controlled Interception) and Sector Control radar services were slowly improving, full blown GCAs (Ground Controlled Approaches with complete glidepath and azimuth positioning information) were for some time only available at the key Master Airfields (later Master Diversion Airfields), or the bomber or night fighter airfields, such as Ahlhorn or Gütersloh.

The Standard Operating Procedure (SOP) for recovery of day fighters from upper levels above cloud into low airfield visibility and cloud bases, was by the 'QGH' Controlled Descent Through Cloud (CDTC) let-down. This was by CAD/F (VHF), later CRDF (UHF, Cathode Ray Direction Finding) ATC positioning, for fighter pairs to be fed on to differently monitored 'stepdown' ACR 7 (azimuth horizontal positioning without glidepath slope information) airfield control radar approaches, sometimes referred to as 'poor man's GCA'. CAD/F Approach Controllers on the ground could note the vector of the aircraft relative to overhead base, whenever the aircraft made R/T contact at altitude. DME (Distance Measuring Equipment), at several station sites only, could assist pilots' fixing of their position at altitude, the monitoring of overheads being given. If a DME was at one's base, a pilot could produce a self-help, bastardised final approach let-down with CAD/F if ACR 7 equipment went unserviceable.

Initial approach to start a 'QGH descent' meant, from operating fighter altitudes of above 45,000 ft., a calculated free, safe and 'flood flow'* clear weather descent, into R/T contact with one's base Approach controller, for an identified arrival into the overhead. A confirmatory level turn followed next, in the overhead at Flight Level 200 (20,000

ft. once QFE pressure was set for let-down) or at another pre-selected safe altitude separation. Usually Hunters would be in spaced paired sub sections, with delayed descents on to their outbound headings for safe separation and control.

Descent from the 'overhead cone' would be at 300 knots with 23 degrees of flap ('2 notches'), 6,500 rpm set and with airbrakes selected out, once cleared to descend outbound. This heading would be an offset teardrop, outbound reciprocal to the runway in use, with an appropriate allowance made for the wind effect in the descent and the right or left hand turn. Ideally this would pre-position pairs rolling out, again inbound, on the extended centreline to level at about 3,500 ft. and 8 to 10 miles out; then, with undercarriages being lowered below 250 kts and the aircraft checked for 'three greens', as appropriate through 2,000 ft. or so, down to an established key 1,500 ft. platform. At, say, 6 miles out, dwindling to five and a half miles, one would be steadied with landing checks completed before commencing the final descent with full flap selected. Leaders, by hand and nodded execution signals for each of the spaced pairs of aircraft minimised the use of R/T.

For Hunter pairs (more so with the later heavier FGA.9s and FR.10s) this would often mean a dribbled fraction of more power to settle on to the final 'stepdown' approach at 5 miles from the threshold, at a nominal descent rate of 750 ft./minute, losing 300 ft. per mile, at 155kts depending on weight, turbulence, wind gradients and the finally called surface wind. Corrective headings to steer for adjustments in the changing winds would be called out by the controller, as well as the appropriate heights for the distances being called ('you should now be passing through x hundred feet' etc.). Break off limits for theoretical diversions were linked to Instrument Rating Cards held (Master Green, Green, White, or Unrated). Threshold speed at normal weights and conditions would be 135 kts and the Hunter was a most reassuring aircraft to fly down on bad weather approaches, both for leaders and 'number twos'.

Obviously mutual practice was as necessary for both controllers and pilots, with full GCA allowing greater precision down to much lower break off limits. On encountering severe weather deterioration, with 2TAF diversions invariably distant, pilots would often have to add (or more accurately subtract!) a modicum of judgement on safety limits, particularly if there was a stack of other Hunters behind or ahead trying to recover to the same airfield.

The most obvious, if subtle, external difference between the Hunter F.4 and F.6 was the upswept tapering tail cone of the former, clearly seen in this excellent shot of F.4 XE668 'G' of 26 Sqn taxiing at Oldenburg in October 1956. (H.Weichardt)

* *Boosting cockpit canopy and windscreen air pre-heating, found particularly necessary after a long time spent at low temperature and high altitudes, followed by rapid clear weather descents into high relative humidity lower air - most Hunter pilots, forgetting their 'flood flow' selection first, would only ever experience this low fuel, low altitude inconvenience of being totally misted up the once, particularly having to move into close formation near the ground, after a satisfyingly rapid descent, from eight miles up, straight on to the centreline!*

Scramble times and 'Trade', normal and clandestine: On 7 April '58 at Jever, with No.4 (AC) Sqn. I have one Battle Flight scramble time noted, when paired with Dickie Barraclough, when we recorded 2 minutes and 33 seconds - this was from an actual scramble from the upstairs crewroom to one's aircraft personally prepared, checked, with parachute and security harnesses laid waiting and alert crews - this was a good time for that long parallel taxy track to airborne. We were at '5 minutes readiness' - a respectable three and a half minutes was normal from squawk box notification in 'Shiny Four's first floor crewroom to 'wheels up'. The normal 2TAF 1957-59 cine interception diet (one needed two seconds of killing film to justifiably claim; it was very bad form to claim incorrectly, even more so of other Hunters on desperately fly through shots etc.) would be any mix of F-100, F-86, Packets, the odd Ouragan or even Mystere, plenty of Canadian and a few Belgian CF-100's, T-33s, the odd F-84 and many RF-84Fs and on Ex. Amleds and others, Canberras galore - we would see and attack unmolested quite a few B-66s and once I claimed a B-57, plus the very first 2ATAF claim on 6 April, 1959 of a F-102 within days of their arrival.

V-Bomber Interceptions, particularly, if we were using the anti-jamming Green Salad equipment were always great fun, as I note we were majoring on in 'Exercise Fullplay' in June 1958 with Valiants. The beauty of the V-Bombers, particularly the Victor and Vulcan, in a late evening or early morning sky could only be described as truly ethereal. Our experimenting with unorthodox type attacks from well ahead and below on pull up firing attacks, with flap at the last minute, must have caused raised eyebrows, if they had ever been seen.

Among interesting if frustrating Battle Flight scramble sorties were those when we would see a glint above us 30 or 40 miles away, just before a new and most authoritative voice would suddenly break in and turn us most firmly and promptly away from these 'clandestine inbounds', which we never discussed too much but obviously knew

Selection of Alan Pollock's ciné gun camera photo's, top to bottom: Hunter, closer than normal 150 yd break off range; F-102 seeks escape in afterburner; contrailing Valiant, Ex 'Topweight' 16.4.59

what was going on, with a 'rather them than us' feeling decades later, we would discover that some of them might well have been among those earlier posted 2TAF colleagues.

Operational Turnrounds The 'just possible' 10 minutes refuel and re-arm 'Operational Turnround from touch down to taxy out for next sortie' was one of the Hunter's finest attributes; waved into dispersal and facing an APC sand revetment or safe area over the airfield, the pilot shuts down his Hunter, rapidly double chocked amid a blur of eager armourers. The procedural maze of orders, grunts and shouts of the turnround team coalesce into the race of refuellers, riggers, engine mechs, instrument bashers and electricians, all in one converging swarm of activity around, below, level and above one's gaze. The ladder is up and ejection pins are in, as that other last symphonic engine whine and wind-down reaches one's ears in the open cockpit with the combined throttle and High Pressure Cock already off that hauntingly distinctive desyncopated Avon music clatters into its finale swirl of ever looser compressor blades and cooling hot metal jet pipe - noisier lower revolutions drop back to a quietened nought. One's arms are already up and out, clearly in view of the canopy coming, as one shouts (guns) 'all switches safe' - the wheel well arming circuit safety break plug and flag hanging down are made safe as the front panel drops as fuses are held up. The

empty forked trolley comes in, Sabrina panels are down, grounded with a soft aluminium scraping and ammo links clinking to be emptied; the fuselage attachment jack drop point spindles, port and starboard, are fixed in - barrels have already been unlocked, with winches now hooked on and in, the removable gun pack is crack- released and wire-wound down, initially with that slightly drunken sway, one way or the other, after the first few inches of ratchet drop takes its weight, eventually nestling onto the quick-kick-adjusted low semicircular cradle, for it to settle, barely a second before it is wheeled out and into a turn. A new gunpack and cradle is soon back in, under, and on its way upwards, accompanied by the whir of ratchets as the armourers winch the new pack into position. As the pack comes flush with the fuselage surface a crisp whipcrack announces that the torque limiters have been exceeded - the barrels are already being twist-locked into place. More scurrying and watching for the bowser's hose to be removed, oxygen replenished and trolley gone, starter cartridges (or later, AVPIN) topped up, with the engine checks and turnround completed, and own pre-starting checks as a last look around. A Form 700 is thrust into the cockpit with a smile and a biro beneath one's nose, as you click in a new ciné magazine and ejection seat pins are removed and stowed. Ready to start, thumbs up acknowledged, and all under eight minutes or so - can't be bad; press tit and the cartridge fires (or that acrid, pungent hiss in the case of the F.6's Avpin), and we're cooking again with Avtur... and ready to be on our way. The after-start checks in seconds, radio taxy call, brakes off and check curtsy, and off we go; we'll make 10-11 minutes from touchdown to take off this time - fancy actually being paid to do this as one's routine day job!

Fg Off Alan Pollock when a very young first tour pilot with 26 Sqn at Oldenburg standing beside the tail of his Hunter F.4, and carrying his white bone dome, beautifully decorated with the Squadron's Springbok emblem. (Alan Pollock)

Dick Barraclough
(118 & 4 Sqns)

By the end of April 1957 I had been on 118 Squadron at RAF Jever for eighteen months and had flown 300 hours on the Hunter 4; at about this time we learned that 118 was to be disbanded at the end of August and that I would be joining 4 Squadron as 'B' Flight Commander. I first flew a Mark 6 on 3 May '57 and remember that I was checked out by Lt. (RN) Bob Parkinson on 4 Sqn; I don't remember whether this came about because I was going to join 4, who had just equipped with 6s or because Bob was a good chum! Three differences from the Mk.4 were apparent to me during that 40 minute flight, firstly the start was Avpin as opposed to cartridge which was basically similar but required slightly different timing in the event of a non-start. Also the handling in the air was significantly improved by the more powerful engine combined with the 'saw tooth' leading edge which increased the rate of turn. The aircraft I flew then was clean but although it had not fitted wing tanks to the Mk.4 it became standard with the Mk.6 to do so

A superb echelon formation of 118 Sqn F.4s comprising, left to right, XE682 'Z', WW651 'G', WT748 'S', led by WT743 'R' flown by (then) Flt Lt Ken Goodwin. (Ken Goodwin via Andy Thomas)

and this to a degree offset the advantage gained by the increased power and extended leading edge.

I flew a 4 Sqn. Mk.6 three more times during May culminating in a sortie on Battle Flight and formed the opinion that it was a worthy successor to the F.4 although initially at least I remember we did not get the same excellent serviceability. This was due partly to the engine fuel system and to the introduction of radar ranging. In the latter case we flew with unserviceable radar ranging for some time in order to prove all the other aspects of this new mark but it became apparent that unless we tested the radar ranging as an essential component we would not be able to rely on it. This decision resulted in another drop in serviceability but eventually brought about a rapid improvement in radar ranging servicing.

In September 1957 we took part in Exercise Brown Jug from Schleswigland, (now the Luftwaffe base of Jagel) where we were accommodated in tents (probably the last time that 2 TAF deployed as such). During this exercise we flew low level sorties of 1 hour duration with wing tanks as opposed to the 40 minute sortie at low level on the Mk.4. This exercise was followed after Christmas by a Sylt

detachment for air-to-air gunnery where the scores, particularly at high level, which had previously been moderate, were much improved and the Squadron produced record results.

Later in 1958 we got the opportunity to evaluate the Hunter 6 against the Sabre 6 when we went to Soellingen to join the RCAF there. They did little low level work but were experts at high level intercepts and air-to-air combat, both singly and in large formations. We concluded that the Hunter was superior in speed and acceleration, although the extended leading edge did not give us as good a rate of turn as the 'soft' wing Sabre. However, our advantage was absolute at height and in closing speed; as long as this was not thrown away by turning with a Sabre for more than about 90 degrees it could be maintained throughout an engagement. The two aircraft had a similar range but the Hunter's reaction time due to its starting system was markedly less than the Sabre. From an operational readiness platform we could be airborne in less than a minute.

During this detachment interesting tactics evolved when we combined Hunters and Sabres against Sabres; we would have four Sabres in battle formation with four Hunters 5,000 ft. above them. When the Sabres were attacked the Hunters had no difficulty in diving down to engage the attacking Sabres, often getting into firing range before they were seen. All very satisfactory!

Gordon Browne *(3 Sqn.)*

Lucky 13: Virtually all my flying has been on single engined jets or pistons. Although this makes life comparatively simple (only one go-faster lever), it does mean that if Messrs Rolls Royce, Armstrong Siddeley or any other maker's product cannot take the strain, then things tend to go very quiet. This is a tale of one such incident, one of many suffered by that classic aircraft, the Hunter.

The early days of the Hunter were not trouble-free. It was rumoured that to be declared operational on the F.2 equipped squadron at RAF Wattisham, you had to have done at least one real forced landing! The problem of engine surge and/or flame out at high level was solved by introducing an automatic fuel dipping system which meant that, at the critical moment in a dog fight, you suddenly lost 1,000 pounds of push. Also, if you pulled a little too hard in the thin air at high altitude, the leading set of static blades of the compressor could flutter, touch the first row of rotating blades and - blatt! - you have stripped the compressor down to the blade roots.

13th May 1957 was a typical Spring day at RAF Geilenkirchen the southernmost airfield in the soon to be

4 Sqn C.O. Sqn Ldr J. Ray Chapman seated centre, with Lt Bob Parkinson on his right, one of the few Royal Navy exchange pilots to serve on Hunter squadrons in Germany. The photograph was taken in early May 1957, in the period before fairly diminutive squadron markings were added to the nose of the new Hunter F.6s. Note the tail support strut. (Ray Chapman)

demolished 2TAF. Just one month before, Duncan Sandys had produced his infamous Defence White Paper and nine of the thirteen Hunter squadrons and all the Venom units in Germany had gone or were awaiting disbandment. As a very wet behind the ears first tourist I had only joined 3(F) Squadron (the first RFC squadron to fly heavier than air machines) in the previous November. Our boss, Squadron Leader Tim Hutchinson, decreed that, until the Benson Ferry Wing pilots' arrival, we would get every last hour we could, and attempt to drain the Officers' Mess stocks of Carlsberg. After a weekend heavily involved in the latter noble cause, we assembled to continue the former.

My first trip was a singleton general handling sortie finishing off with three practice forced landings, this was continuing a trial of a new way of bringing home your broken jet. Developed, I believe, by the Fleet Air Arm, the new pattern only required a good overhead to be given and then, making use of the excellent glide of a clean Hunter, punching down at high speed to below the cloud. If you got it right, you could come down to a 1,000 feet base and still leave room to either eject safely or land. As I signed in after the sortie, I noticed that it was my 12th trip of the month so far and the 12th successful test of the new force landing pattern.

The next trip was to be a routine four ship battle formation fighter sweep into 4ATAF airspace; I was flying No.2 to the flight leader, Peter Vangucci. Our standard ploy was to climb to about 20,000 feet to the north of Geilenkirchen then turn south so that we would be at 40,000 + feet before entering 'hostile' airspace. For months we had been hassling with the USAF F-100's and the RCAF Sabre 6s based in southern Germany and north eastern France. The Sabre 6 was the most dangerous - the Canadian pilots were far more experienced and the '6/3' wing of the Sabre gave it the edge over the Hunter F.4 at high altitude.

Sure enough, somewhere over the cloud-covered Eifel hills came the call - '8 at 6 o'clock climbing'. We turn hard into the threat - watch the power setting - (ever hopeful of catching the Sabre on cine!) tighten up to hold position on Peter - Bang! RPM falling, jet pipe temperature (JPT) rising must be a surge. Throttle back and dive below 30,000 feet - 'Nailcream Black Two engine surge descending to 30 thou to sort it'. 'Nailcream Black Two - Roger. I'm behind you'. 30,000 feet, speed below 300 knots, um, max RPM available only 6,200 (should be 7,800), JPT a bit high, no sign of any push. The penny drops. To prevent stator and first stage compressor blades touching at high revs and angle of attack, Rolls Royce had introduced 'Mod 441', increasing the gap between the rows of blades by a quarter of an inch. Earlier this month Bob 'Leadfoot' Hillman had had a similar failure. I wonder - yup dear ol' B Bravo was unmodified.

So here we are at about 29,000 feet somewhere over a cloud-covered Eifel, rpm 6200, no thrust, speed to glide at 230 knots - about 1,600 feet a minute rate of descent. No idea where the nearest airfield is and Pete can't help as he doesn't know either. Oh well: *'Mayday, Mayday, Mayday'.*

A rather bored, heavily accented America voice answers: *'Nailcream Black Two, this is Yellowjack* (the 4ATAF emergency fixer service). *We hear your Mayday but are unable to assist you at this time'.* To pre-date Victor Meldrew by many years: 'I don't believe it'. 25,000 feet and still nothing but cloud and the odd glimpse of German pine trees. Then, faintly, a Canadian voice *'Nailcream Black this is Marville we have a slow moving target 075, 40 miles steer 255 for ident'* - hope at last. 2 miles per 1,000 feet is the rule of thumb so should just make it.

The ruined engine is still running, giving hydraulics and electrics. Marville's voice gets louder as I glide down now in and out of the stratocumulous cover. *'Cloud base 6/8 at 1,500 you are advised to eject.'* Stuff that. Finally, joy of joys, a runway, well the up-wind half anyway. Hydraulics still OK but remember Bob lost his engine in the last few seconds on finals, so prepare to blow down the wheels and flaps and revert to manual. Three Greens - keep the speed up round finals - aiming high because full flap really dumps you, like now! Full flap, over the threshold at 140- and the engine finally dies. Let it roll - sign of fire wagons - touch of brake and turn off at the 2000 yard mark. Made it. Pins in the seat, climb out to be met by a grinning fireman *'Sir, you have one very silvery jet pipe'*. He's right, all that lovely metal melted and sprayed down the full length. A more senior Canadian, the Wing Commander Flying, demanded to know why I had done a dead stick in a cloud base of only 1500 feet. Their SOP was 5,000 feet minimum or eject. They still had the very inefficient US designed seat not that greatest life saver, the Martin Baker.

So that was it - almost. After a suitably alcoholic spree with the Canadians of No.441 Squadron and others, Les Elgey picked me up in a Vampire T.11 and we returned to find the other '13s'. My sortie in the authorisation sheet was the 13th as the duty authoriser had forgotten to write 12A. It was also the 13th pre-mod 441 failure in the Command. I should have stayed in bed.

Afterwards, Les Elgey went back to collect 'B' with its new engine. 441 Squadron had got at it and resprayed it in their well known black and white checks with maple leafs in the roundels. We kept the checks but quickly removed the maple leafs because, as Tim Hutchinson said, we are combating nations.

In 1964 when flying Gnats at RAF Valley we were searching for a name for the first Gnat aerobatic team. Flight Lieutenant Lee Jones, the leader, and I were swapping stories over a beer. Why not Yellowjack I suggested, Lee had had a similar experience with that organisation a few weeks before my episode. So 'Yellowjack' they became - I still prefer it to the 'Red Arrows'. And the moral? Black cats, walking under ladders or one 13 take it in your stride. Two or three 13s - take care. But four 13s is too much even for a Rolls Royce!

Reproduced from 'Forever Aircrew', reminiscences of members of the Hereford and The Marches Branch of the Air Crew Association.

Gordon Browne's Hunter 4 XF976 'B' of 3 Sqn at Marville after his emergency landing and its subsequent decoration with black and white checks, courtesy of resident 441 Sqn RCAF, which flew Sabre 6s at the time. (Gordon Browne)

Nigel Walpole *(26 & 2 Sqns.)*

My two Hunter tours in Germany were very different, from being a junior pilot on Hunter F.4 day fighters, with No.26 (AC) Squadron at RAF Oldenburg in the mid-1950s, to squadron commander of No.II (AC) Squadron on fighter reconnaissance (FR) with the Hunter FR. 10 at RAF Gütersloh, ten years later. Most of our work in the day fighter business had been carried out in the upper airspace (although in my latter days at Oldenburg we were practising 'rat and terrier' tactics at low level), whereas the FR role called for training At the lowest levels permitted. Unique among the NATO tactical reconnaissance squadrons, we regularly rehearsed the use of the Hunter's four, very effective 30 mm cannon, in air-to-air so that we might be prepared to fight our way in or out of the target area, and air-to-ground for use against high value targets on the ground. Of course we would put our primary reconnaissance tasks first, where possible avoiding a fight or placing these missions at risk in lower priority ground attack. In both modes the gunnery results we achieved compared very well with those of the fighter/ground attack squadrons.

The two Hunter FR squadrons in Germany in the 1960s (Nos. II and 4)

Another Hunter 4 with a bare metal tail cone, this time WV255 'X' of 26 Sqn, the 'personal' aircraft of Flt Lt Nigel Walpole, at Oldenburg in November 1956. (H.Weichardt)

worked to the same training syllabus, but their respective COs were allowed some discretion on how they met these requirements. The undoubted and very visible prestige to be gained in peacetime from success in the national and NATO reconnaissance competitions (Sassoon and Royal Flush) encouraged academic excellence more than operational imperatives - and the priorities accorded to each changed with time and incumbents.

During my time, II Squadron tried to simulate operational conditions as closely as possible. In war, we would have been tasked predominantly as single aircraft, for economy of effort and because the mutual support of a pair was unrealistic at the very very low levels we intended to fly, with high-'g' manoeuvring in the terrain (especially that in the Sauerland and Harz mountains) and poor weather we had to expect. However, in training we often flew in pairs, adopting measures which put both pilots under stress. Such sorties were usually flown on the standard 'trip of the day' typically over three targets, maybe a line search, bridge and a camouflaged military target in the field - the latter arranged by our army Ground Liaison Officer (GLO). In line astern,

`01S(15)` `2 RAF 7853 22AUG69 1200Z 4 IN 500FT EX SOUTHERN RANGER NATO RESTRICTED`

both pilots would be required to photograph the targets and gather information visually for the in-flight reports and independent written reports after landing. In many cases these activities were carried out against the clock. The project officer might then add further pressure by issuing covert briefings on a change of lead or an in-flight task - perhaps tasking a 'bounce' aircraft to disrupt the mission en route. At the end of each day, the Photographic Interpreter (PI) and the GLO would display all the mission results in a mass de-briefing. This type of operational training offered a fair basis for comparison and an on-going evaluation of individual performance, with an incentive to improve, while removing any temptation to resort to less operational ways.

When the weather was not suitable for low flying, the choice was between a ground training programme, conserving flying hours and helping to recover unserviceable aircraft, or of climbing above cloud for combat training and other upper air work. II Squadron invariably chose the latter, to improve aircraft handling generally and develop skills which might enhance survival in war. Within contingency plans, weekend forays to Denmark and Norway on Exercise Blue Diamond, and to Italy, Malta and North Africa on Exercise Southern Ranger, gave the pilots some insight into other operating environments.

Exploiting the aircraft's versatile capability to the full, the Hunter FR. 10 force in Germany proved itself 'second to none' (II (AC) Squadron's unofficial motto).

Grand Harbour, Valletta, Malta forms the impressive backdrop to this super study of 2 Sqn Hunter FR.10 XF432 'S', photographed from the accompanying wing-man as they overfly the island at 500 feet. It bears testimony to the quality of the F.95 cameras with which the FR.10 was equipped. The Squadron Leader's pennant and pilot's name below the cockpit identifies Sqn Ldr T. Barrett, and the pilot's bone dome also carries 2 Sqn markings. (Nigel Walpole)

E.L. `Peter' McMillan
(135 Wing Leader, RAF Brüggen)

The following contribution from Group Captain 'Peter' McMillan, CBE, AFC explains how he acquired the soubriquet 'Mayday Mac' while he was Brüggen Wing Leader.

My first connection with Brüggen began in 1951 while I was at the Ministry where I joined a team that was sent to Paris to discuss with the French, Americans, and Canadians the location of four new NATO airfields that would be needed in West Germany, one of which turned out to be Brüggen.

In 1955 I returned to England from the Middle East to go to Northern Sector at Linton-on-Ouse. One day in February 1956 a Staff Officer in Fighter Command rang me up to ask if I would like to take over the Wing at Brüggen; it seemed that they were about to convert from Sabres to Hunters. In spite of my total lack of day fighter experience this was an offer I could not refuse, so I converted on to Hunters at 233 OCU, Pembrey. In fairness it should be said that in his report the Wing Commander Flying said that my proposed appointment was quite unsuitable in view of my (night fighter) background. Nevertheless I went out to Brüggen and took over 135 Wing in April 1956. I imagine the Station Commander, Group Captain A.G. (Tony) Dudgeon wondered what he was getting!

The Wing was in the process of converting to the Hunter F.4, and flying consisted of getting used to the aircraft, interception practice and ground attack. The Group Headquarters had a very cautious approach to bad weather flying, which was not surprising, because the weather information from the west was very indifferent. There had been a number of occasions where these short duration aircraft had been caught out and had been lucky to get down at one or other of our four airfields. With the advice and agreement of the four squadron commanders we arranged to send up a recce. aircraft each morning to the west to report on the weather coming in, and this seemed to be effective. At the same time there appeared to be a reluctance to practice night flying, but my experience in this field helped to overcome this attitude.

I was pretty bad at formation flying, but that did not matter as I was always the leader and the others had to fly on me. We were asked to do a number of flypasts for dignitaries visiting Wildenrath, and they went quite well. On 14 October 1956 we were asked to

Brüggen-based Hunter F4 XF318 'Z' of 130 Sqn with the unusual unpainted rear fuselage. (via Geoff Cruikshank)

do a flypast for Princess Alice, Duchess of Gloucester; we therefore carried out a rehearsal on 12 October and this was satisfactory. I can't remember exactly how many aircraft were involved, but it was intended to be the whole Wing so there would have been at least 32 in the formation.

We had a satisfactory weather forecast before we took off The procedure was to form up after take-off under the surveillance of the radar, but on this occasion shortly after take-off the weather clamped, and when I tried to lead the formation back to Brüggen it was clear we would not be able to make it, and in fact the only airfield open was Wahn.

Rightly or wrongly I sent out a Mayday call and split the formation into its component parts. These sections were brilliantly handled by the air traffic controller at Wahn who was later awarded a much deserved Queen's Commendation. All the aircraft landed safely, the last one being the Station Commander.

The next day we attempted another flypast from Wahn, but ground control had the aircraft confused, and the flypast had to be aborted, and it was not until 17th October that it was successfully concluded.

(Above) Line up of 112 Sqn Hunters at Brüggen (Robin Brown)

(Below) 67 Sqn F.4 XF317 at Brüggen early '56. Code letter 'U' is pale blue and repeated on the nose door (via Peter Caygill)

A formation flypast by 16 Hunter 4s over the RAF ensign at the saluting base. In fact those depicted are components of the Jever Wing, but such sizeable Hunter formations were by no means unusual in Germany in 1955-57. (Ray Chapman)

Mick Ryan (93 Sqn.)
Battle Flight Incident at RAF Jever

In 1959 I was at Jever on 93 Squadron and I remembered an exciting incident when, for the first time, I really thought I was going to war. Recently, I was checking up with Pete Jennings who was on 4 Squadron at the time, to see if he could remember any details. To my delight he told me that he was the leader of the Battle Flight pair and he remembered the occasion very well. His number two was John Farley, who later became famous as the test pilot that developed the Harrier. The rest of the story is as Pete told it to me.

When it was RAF Jever's turn for Battle Flight duty, it was practice to mount two armed Hunters, (at that time), on the flight line in front of the hangar. The ejection seats were prepared for rapid strapping in and all the checks were done so that all the pilot had to do was press the start button once he was cleared by the ground crew. Then he finished strapping in, obtained take-off clearance and taxied out to the duty runway for a rolling take off. While on duty two pilots were allowed to wait in the Squadron Operations room in the hangar, and the scramble came through on the squawk box. They were allowed 5 minutes to get airborne.

At the end of the duty period, the Battle Flight pair was often scrambled as a training exercise. This was just as they handed over to the night fighters and it meant that the two pilots did get some flying for that day. However this was never done in poor weather.

Sunday 6 December 1959 was a miserable day, bad fog and no forecast of improvement. It was 4 Squadron's turn for Battle Flight duty and the first pair on was Pete and John. The rest of the single pilots were lounging around the Mess either trying to get over the night before or still asleep in bed. The married aircrew were at home doing whatever married aircrew do on a Sunday morning - washing the car and the children.

Pete checked in with the Duty Flight Authorising Officer, Mike Tyrell, and made it clear that he didn't expect Brockzetel, our Sector Operations Control Radar Station just down the road, to try any silly antics like test scrambling Battle Flight. Jever, along with every other airfield in Germany, was 'Red', i.e. the weather was too bad for flying. A scramble would probably end in an ejection over the North Sea and, at best, a ride home in the RAF Air Sea Rescue Launch.

About an hour into their duty period the Squawk Box announced a scramble. Pete and John were not impressed but duly got airborne. John rolled in formation with Pete, who was flying XJ637, and stayed with him until they

93 Sqn Battle Flight, with F.6s XJ645 'E' and XE550 'R' at readiness at Jever, spring 1959. These are still in early markings, and without later mods. (Mick Ryan)

were on top of the fog. The alternative was to wait until Pete was airborne and join up on top, usually a messy business. They were given a south east vector and climbed to 30,000 ft.

We in the Mess were not aware of the full meteorological picture but were still surprised to hear the two Hunters scrambled in that visibility. We slumped back in to reading the newspapers or sleeping and the next pair raced round the airfield to take over stand-by. The next 4 Squadron pair lined up were Whisky Walker, later to become a very senior RAF Officer, and a Flt Lt Anderson, who's Christian name I cannot remember.

After a while the second pair scrambled. The Mess exploded - no one scrambled two Battle Flight pairs unless it was very serious, particularly in view of the weather. I remember I was reasonably dressed and drove straight to 93 Squadron, the other resident Hunter F.6 squadron at Jever, I was in the next pair up on the line with Joe Parker my Flight Commander leading. I really thought my moment had come.

The rest of the station went into top gear, as it was a war alert. The RAF fire engines were sent down to Jever town to alert all the aircrew and personnel who lived in quarters there. As aircrew arrived on the line, dressed in anything they could put on, (some very fetching pyjamas led to some leg pulling later

on), they were briefed, paired up with anyone as and when they arrived, regardless of which squadron they were from, and went on the line. Standardisation was pretty good even in those days and we all used well understood SOPs. The ground crews were crash arming the Hunters as fast as they could load the ammunition panniers.

Even 2 Squadron pilots, who normally flew Swifts, were being strapped into Hunters as they arrived. Not as crazy as it sounds (and I shall deny having said this), they were the fighter world's most experienced pilots and all had many hours on the Hunter before being selected to join 2 Squadron. The Swift low level reconnaissance role was particularly demanding.

In the meantime, Pete and John were told to descend to about 5,000 ft. still flying south east. They were told

93 Sqn F.6 XE550 'R', summer 1960, with yellow wing tips, and the name of Flt. Lt. Paddy Hine above the nose markings. Pilots, left to right are: Barry Tonkinson, Jeremy Hall, Val Ventham, Tom Ashwood, Pete Bouch, Pete Raeburn, Chris Stone (Flt. Cdr.), Sqn Ldr Olaf Burg (C.O.), Paddy Hine (Flt Cdr.), Mick Ryan (Adjutant), Timber Wood, Colin Lamont, Oscar Wilde, Dennis Fahey, Brian Butterworth. (Mick Ryan)

Hunter 6 XG257 'C' of 93 Sqn, complete with extended cartridge chutes and gun blast deflectors; the pilot is Flt Lt Mick Ryan, whose name is painted above the squadron markings, with '93 Squadron' beneath them, in each instance in yellow on a blue strip, while the Union Jack is on the nose. (Mick Ryan)

that there were five or six targets, first they were to the left and then immediately to the pair's right. Pete was viewing this quite seriously and remembers breaking the sealing wire on the drop down 30 mm Aden gun trigger on the top of his Hunter's control column.

After a while of searching at low level, in and out of the cloud and finding nothing, they were instructed to turn west and climb back up to 20,000 ft. At this point they realised that they were near Erfurt, about 30 nautical miles over the border and inside East Germany. Pete remembers that he was quite rude to John Farley about John's observations on the 'collective farms' he could see down below. Pete was rather hoping John was covering his arse and not sight seeing.

Radar vectored them back through the most southerly of the three airway corridors that ran from West Germany into Berlin. To Pete's surprise he was passed very close to a Polish airliner minding its own business in the airway. He elected to fly behind the airliner rather than cause an international incident by flying across its bows.

He was directed back towards RAF Gütersloh, the home of 14, 20, and 26 Hunter F.6 squadrons, which to their relief, was the only airfield in West Germany to be expediently re-graded to Yellow 3, the lowest meteorological rating that would allow an approach attempt. After a 50 minute flight the pair landed uneventfully at Gütersloh.

As Pete taxied in and unstrapped he was surprised to see that they were being met by a very friendly civilian in a Land Rover. This turned out to be Group Captain Ronnie Knott, Station Commander of RAF Gütersloh, who

proceeded to take them to the bar for a memorable and rare occasion when the Jever and Gütersloh Hunter crews were able to meet socially.

Shortly after landing at Gütersloh, they were joined by Whisky Walker's second Battle Flight pair. Anderson's Hunter refused to retract its undercarriage after take-off and so they had to divert to Gütersloh. Thankfully, the panic subsided and Joe and I were not required in the third Battle Flight pair and Jever stood down and went back for a liquid Sunday lunch in the Mess.

During the wash up it transpired that the southern radars were often bothered by spurious ghost paints suggesting that Warsaw Pact aircraft were flying towards the border and were about to penetrate NATO airspace. The Russians had a habit of doing this, particularly in bad weather, just to test how well our Battle Flight reflexes operated.

On one such occasion, when the weather was equally poor, they flew about 18 helicopters in pairs, across the West German border. Of course, by the time Battle Flight aircraft arrived they had retreated back across the border.

However, Pete told me that it turned out that this was not the cause of his incident. It was finally decided that the returns were from East German trains, moving faster than the MTI (Moving Target Indicator) setting on the West's radar and showing up as flashes as the train presented different facades to the NATO radars.

Swansong

The last influx into RAF Germany of a sizeable number of Hunters was unexpected. It was the consequence of a Buccaneer accident in February 1980 near Nellis AFB, USA in which the aircraft broke up in mid-air.

As the cause of the accident could not be established immediately but fatigue thought to be one of the most likely reasons, the whole Buccaneer force was grounded. To keep the air and ground crews at 15 and 16 Sqns at Laarbruch in current practice, additional Hunters were flown in from the UK and by April 1980, the total number had risen to 12: 4 single seat F. 6s, and 8 two seat T.7s and T.7As.

This number was kept more or less throughout 1980 and the last of the additional aircraft had left by the middle of 1981. When the Buccaneers returned to flying, they kept their "normal" complement of Hunter two seaters until they were disbanded in 1984. From 1982, though, these remaining Hunters had been serviced by the Laarbruch Station Flight. The last aircraft, T.7A WV 318, left the base on 9 March 1984.

Not for the first time towards the end of its service life, the Hunter had been able to fill a gap. That this happened so close to the end of its career in Germany seems to be an appropriate swansong of a superb aircraft and the people who worked with it.

Two Hunter T.7s used at Laarbruch in the Spring of 1982, (top) WV318 with 15 Sqn markings, and XL616 (ex-RAE), each displaying the small penguin marking on the nose, applied by the Laarbruch Servicing Section. (W. Zetsche)